DEVOTIONS FOR MY
Single Mom Life

REBECCA LIST-BERGERON

HARVEST HOUSE PUBLISHERS
EUGENE, OREGON

Cover design by Dugan Design Group, Bloomington, MN

Cover photos © ZUBKOVA IULIIA / Fotolia

Devotions for My Single Mom Life

Copyright © 2019 by Rebecca List-Bergeron
Published by Harvest House Publishers
Eugene, Oregon 97408

www.harvesthousepublishers.com

ISBN 978-0-7369-7516-2 (hardcover w/ribbon)
ISBN 978-0-7369-7517-9 (eBook)

Library of Congress Cataloging-in-Publication Data
Names: List-Bergeron, Rebecca, author.
Title: Devotions for my single mom life / Rebecca List-Bergeron.
Description: Eugene : Harvest House Publishers, 2019.
Identifiers: LCCN 2018049668 (print) | LCCN 2018053603 (ebook) | ISBN
  9780736975179 (ebook) | ISBN 9780736975162 (pbk.)
Subjects: LCSH: Single mothers--Religious life. | Single mothers--Prayers and
  devotions.
Classification: LCC BV4529.18 (ebook) | LCC BV4529.18 .L58 2019 (print) | DDC
  242/.6431--dc23
LC record available at https://lccn.loc.gov/2018049668

Printed in the United States of America

19 20 21 22 23 24 25 26 27 / Bang-AR / 10 9 8 7 6 5 4 3 2 1

Acknowledgments

To my parents, Randy and Sug:

Mom, you have inspired me in so many ways. I thank the Lord that you showed me the power of prayer and your passion for the Lord in your life. Even when you walked through the pain of a divorce, your faith remained strong. You have inspired me. I pray that I can be half the mother to my boys that you have been to me. I love you, Mom!

Dad, thank you for loving Mom and us three girls. Thank you for taking on the role of stepdad and loving us. You showed me what a godly marriage looks like. Most of all, I thank you for showing me Jesus in your daily life. I love you, Dad.

To my boys, Caedmen and Eli:

You make me laugh. You challenge me to be more creative, and you always give me something to pray about. You two are my joy, my laughter, my smiles, and my two gifts from God. I cherish the times we have shared. I am so proud to be your mom.

To Jedd:

Where do I even begin? You have walked with me through this whole journey. You've seen it all unfold, and you have encouraged me to keep going even though you knew this was all beyond my comfort zone. You knew, somehow, that this book would bless many single moms out there. You have understood me and believed in me. I can't thank you enough.

To my close friend Shannan, a fellow single mom and artist:

You are the one I can call at any time, even in the middle of the night. I can lean on you for anything, and you have the biggest heart. I love your zeal for life!

To my pastor, Troy, and his wife, Julie:

Thank you for supporting me and all my adventures when I hear God calling me. And thank you for encouraging me to use my talents for the Lord. I am so grateful to call Steamboat Christian Center my home for the past 13 years.

To my dear friend Sue:

Thank you for always seeing my worth, for seeing me through God's eyes, and for always being available to talk and pray with me. Love you, Sue.

To the Harvest House family:

Thank you, Todd Hafer, Gene Skinner, and the whole team for using your many talents to make this book come to life. Harvest House is an instrument used by God to spread light, and I am truly blessed to have the opportunity to work with all of you.

To my hiking partner, Keva:

You came to our family during the time I needed you most, and you were like a ministering angel to me. You were there every step of the way. You heard my prayers to my heavenly Father, and you heard my heartache. I love you, my fur baby.

To all the single moms and other influential women in my life:

You have inspired me more than you could possibly know. You were vulnerable and transparent when you shared your stories with me. You have encouraged me all along this journey we are on together. Special thanks to Mom, Amy, Angie, Jennifer, Michele, Whitney, Leilani, and Denise for your contributions to this book. You all are amazing!

May God bless you. And let's keep believing the best is yet to come!

To all the single moms and dads, I offer a salute to you. I fight for you. I see your sweat, your tears, your sacrifice, your dedication to your children. I see you giving, giving, giving, without a partner to lean on. And I see you growing, growing, growing. I see you becoming stronger in the face of these challenges, and I am inspired by you. And to you, single mom or dad, I dedicate this book.

Contents

Introduction

*T*o be completely honest, writing this devotional has been quite difficult for me. I have always been a transparent person, but writing a book for single moms like me hurled me into new and frightening territory. It's scary to share my innermost thoughts, to share stories without sugarcoating them. To be open, honest, and raw.

As I wrote, I questioned myself: *Who am I to be creating a book like this? What I do I have to say to women who are struggling with all the challenges the single-mom life throws at us every day?*

On some days, I felt as if the answer to the second question was "nothing." But then I realized I was looking at my task the wrong way. I was focused too much on myself and my insecurities. The truth is that if the words of this book touch your heart, encourage you, or comfort you in some way, that's the Lord's work. I want to convey his love and truth as I have experienced them as the single mom of two boys. That's my only prayer, really—that the Lord somehow uses this book to bring more light to the very dark times that many of us experience.

I hope you will see yourself in the stories I share. It's not always easy to share our personal stories. Shame can form such a huge barrier to communication. Believe me, I know.

This, the single-mom life, is not the way most of us wanted things to turn out. We knew that marriage and motherhood would bring both the good and the bad, but we couldn't imagine going through what we have endured. As young married people, who of us looked at a single mom from our neighborhood or our church and thought, *I bet that will be me someday, walking that grueling road of single motherhood*?

But here we are. We try to raise these gifts God has given us. On some days, we don't feel up to the task, but we do the best we can. Alone.

However, are we *really* alone? Throughout my life, I have been surrounded by remarkable women. Women I look up to. Many of these women were (or still are) single moms. They have encouraged me. They have given me wise advice. Most important, they have given of themselves through their time, their stories, and their love.

As I thought about these amazing women, I regained my confidence to write this book. I realized how much I want to encourage you because I know how much that kind of encouragement has meant to me.

I want to share stories, ideas, and activities you can do with your kids. I want to issue a few challenges. I want to give you some biblical passages to meditate on. These Scriptures have given me hope during my darkest days. I pray they will do the same for you.

Most of all, I want you to know this important truth: It's not over! The Lord has a future for you, a future filled with blessings and joy—so much that you'll barely be able to contain yourself. I believe all this goodness will pour over onto our children and even the future generations of our families.

When families break apart, the enemy wants to use that to

destroy us. But God won't allow that. He wants to transform what's broken into something amazing. I know that right now, it might be hard for you to see "amazing." But God's promises are true. Follow him and prepare to be amazed.

Rebecca List-Bergeron

1

Just Breathe

We know that all things work together for good to those
who love God, to those who are the called according to
His purpose.

Romans 8:28 NKJV

*A*s we get started, I want to share a little more about myself and
what the single-mom life looks like for me. I live in northern Colorado with my two wonderful boys, Caedmen and Eli (ages 14
and 11), as well as a gorgeous Siberian husky named Keva.

Keva has been my hiking partner, ministering angel, and listening ear during times of heartbreak. As I write these words,
I have been divorced for two years. My marriage ended after
sixteen years. It was not my decision, not my choice. In fact, I
opposed the divorce. I sought wise counsel, and I pleaded that
my husband and I could find another way. I tried to find *any*
other alternative to divorce.

I remember the pain, the tears, and the questions. How could
this happen to my family? What did I do wrong? Why wasn't I
good enough? Why wasn't I "enough" for him?

I had dreamed about growing old with the man I married. I
compared myself to others, the married women in my church
and my family. And I beat myself up because my story differed
from theirs.

I struggled to find hope.

Meanwhile, God remained faithful through it all.

This doesn't mean I now have the answers to all my questions. I don't. In fact, I might never know the answers to some questions, but I do know who is holding me, my boys, and our future.

As I've been writing, I find myself wishing I could tell you I have arrived. I wish I could tell you everything that was broken has been made whole. Instead, I am striving to be honest on every page. That's one thing you can count on as you read. I battle with my emotions every day. Sometimes I look at my boys and see how sad they are because they don't have a dad around every day. On days like these, all I can do is breathe. *Breathe.* I love that word. I have it written on a poster above my bed. *Breathe*, I often remind myself. *Just breathe.*

A few days ago, I was reflecting on some words written by Amy Axby. Amy is a writer with amazing talents. Her blog, Lady the Fearless, blesses me and so many other people. With Amy's permission, I am sharing some of her unpublished words, words that have truly touched my heart. I pray that they will bless you as well.

Today I'm praying for anyone struggling with anxiety, stress, or worry of any kind.

I'm praying for you to feel a deep, fresh breath in your chest right now. A deep, slow, healing, cleansing breath that fills you with peace, all the way from your chin to your belly.

Inhale love, exhale anxiety.

Inhale love, exhale worry.

Inhale love, exhale stress.

I'm praying for your eyes to be able to shift from the problem to the One who loves you. For you to remember that you are held. He has you in the palm of His hand, no matter what. I pray you can rest in knowing that. I pray you can rest in His love.

I proclaim that all your circumstances are covered by the blood of Jesus. There is nothing that can snatch you out of His hand. There is nothing that He cannot handle. There is nothing that can keep you from His love.

I pray you know that you are not a failure. Everyone makes mistakes, but you are not defined by them. And your future is not a sum total of your mistakes. Someone needs to hear that right now. God is your redeemer. He's already got it figured out.

Breathe.

Breathe.

Breathe.

I pray that the static of anxiety, worry, and stress falls away now, and you see it crumbling under your feet for what it is: a dirty lie sent to keep you from all God has for you.

And I pray for joy to take its place! For laughter! For childlike fun! For trust. For gratitude and vision and wisdom to increase in the place of sneaky fears.

I proclaim that you will not let fear steal from you any

longer. You are done with it. You are resting in His promises, in His love.

God, help us keep our eyes on You, no matter the cir-
cumstance, no matter the storm. We have water to walk on.
We have steps to take.

We trust You to help us in every area and work it all out
for our good. We give You permission to blow the ceiling
off our expectations.

We exhale everything that is not of You, with every
breath! And inhale heaven in its place. We love You, Jesus.
Amen.

I keep this piece on my smartphone, and I turn to these
words when I know I need to spend a few minutes quieting my
heart and breathing deep. On the really challenging days, I find
myself reading these words over and over.

I've talked to lots of single moms while writing this book, and
I've come to realize that we all have different stories. We are at
different places in our journeys. But there is a common theme:
None of our stories are over! The Lord has blessed us with one of
the most important jobs on earth—raising our children. In fact,
this might be *the* most important job on earth for many of us.
This is our task regardless of whether we have positive coparent-
ing relationships with our exes.

Whatever the case, God has so much in store for us and our
kids. I know the Lord is holding me right now. He is holding my
boys and our future, and he is doing the same for you. So breathe.
Just breathe.

"Never be in a hurry; do everything quietly and in a calm spirit. Do not lose your inner peace for anything whatsoever, even if your whole world seems upset."

Saint Francis de Sales

2

Follow the Leader

Wherever your treasure is, there the desires of
your heart will also be.
Matthew 6:21 NLT

As single moms, we see our kids as many things: blessings, challenges, puzzles, and tests of our will and wisdom. But have you ever seen a child as an invitation to worship?

At any age, our kids can help reveal the wonder of God. It's the way a toddler giggles as she waddles across the floor chasing the family dog. Or the way a tattooed teenager stops to hold the door for an elderly couple exiting a coffee shop.

It seems that almost every day, my kids remind me there's nothing ordinary about an "ordinary" day. My kids have helped me realize we are surrounded by miracles. The bee that dances across a fragile crocus petal before nimbly taking flight, carrying half its body weight in pollen. The fat, drifting clouds that look like the faces of bearded Viking warriors. The moon-kissed lake that shines like obsidian underneath the night sky.

My kids have helped me discover, or perhaps rediscover, that the world can be a gallery of masterworks created by a loving Artist.

Like most parents, I spend a lot of time thinking and praying about what and how I should teach my boys. But God has shown me that sometimes I need to become the student. I need to be humble enough to learn from someone who isn't old enough to shave.

Through my sons' eyes, I can see the world around me in fresh and wonderful ways. Notice how Vincent van Gogh delighted in childlike wonder:

> If one feels the need of something grand, something infinite, something that makes one feel aware of God, one need not go far to find it. I think sometimes I see something deeper, more infinite, and more eternal than the ocean in the expression of the eyes of a little baby when it wakes in the morning, and coos or laughs because it sees the sun shining on its cradle.

Realizing my kids have so much to teach me is both humbling and exciting. It makes me eager for each new journey. In the spirit of the great artist Van Gogh, I want to take my kids by the hand (while they'll still let me) and walk with them on paths that will show us the wonder of worship and bring us ever closer to the heart of our loving God.

Father God,
Thank you for all I have discovered (and rediscovered) through my sons' eyes. May I always be open to what you want to teach me, no matter the source of my learning.

Amen.

3

This Too Shall Pass?

Make the most of every opportunity you
have for doing good.
Ephesians 5:16 TLB

*E*very single parent knows that each season of a child's life has its unique joys and pains.

Few moments in life are as precious as cuddling with a tiny baby in your favorite chair. However, hearing that same little one wailing in the middle of the night tries your patience like few other challenges in life.

When my boys were toddlers, their adventurous spirits awakened the child in me time and again. Something *else* was awakened in me when they spilled grape juice on the freshly steam-cleaned rug or smashed a favorite vase.

Today, my boys often surprise me with their clever observations and random acts of extreme kindness. Their sudden outbursts of temper are just as surprising—but not in a good way.

Whenever I have faced a difficult phase of parenting, especially when I first became a single mom, my friends and family would try to console me with this advice: "It's just a phase. It will pass."

I know these people meant well, but I didn't find their words soothing or encouraging. I felt like I was being encouraged to focus on the future instead of what I was experiencing in the moment. The *right now*.

We all know how fast time zips by. It wasn't that long ago that I was rocking my boys to sleep. Flash-forward a few years, and I'm a mom to two adults in the making. Today, more than ever, I don't want to grit my teeth and wait for a difficult stage to pass. I want to live *right now*. I want to savor it all. Even those tough times that drive me to my knees in desperate prayer.

Let's be honest: Parenting is the hardest job in the world. And for those of us who must fly solo much of the time, it's harder still. But I want to be present for it all. The times that challenge my wisdom and patience and the hard-won victories that make me feel like the most fortunate person alive. I want to apologize when I need to. I want to forgive. I want God's perspective on life and parenting. I want to take a deep breath and live every moment.

Whatever phase of parenting you find yourself in, that's where you are. There's no avoiding it. A parenting challenge is not something you rush through with your nose plugged. You jump in and live it. And ideally, you can slow down long enough to look for the unique treasures and life lessons God provides, even in times of crisis or chaos.

As single moms, let's make every moment count. Let's live each one with joy, courage, curiosity, and gratitude.

> *Heavenly Father,*
> *May I remember always that even though I am*
> *called a single parent, I don't parent alone. You are*

surely by my side, even when I am not aware of it. You provide strength, comfort, and courage. Most of all, you provide love. Healing, empowering love. I thank you for that precious gift.

Amen.

4

On Wisdom and Discernment

My child, never drift off course from these two goals for your life:
to walk in wisdom and to discover discernment.
Don't ever forget how they empower you.
For they strengthen you inside and out
and inspire you to do what's right;
you will be energized and refreshed by the healing they bring.
They give you living hope to guide you,
and not one of life's tests will cause you to stumble.
You will sleep like a baby, safe and sound—
your rest will be sweet and secure.
You will not be subject to terror, for it will not terrify you.
Nor will the disrespectful be able to push you aside,
because God is your confidence in times of crisis,
keeping your heart at rest in every situation.
Proverbs 3:21-26 TPT

A "heart at rest in every situation." That is a favorite phrase from these verses in Proverbs. I have prayed this Scripture over my sons since they were babies.

This passage brings me such peace because like most parents, I have often wished I could go back in time and change things I did or said. I wish for a re-do, just one more chance to make things right.

Many of the single moms I talk with feel the same way. However, is it possible that we walked through those "times of crisis" so that we could be where we are *right now*, able to impart wisdom to our children? Maybe they are facing a similar crisis, or maybe they will in the future.

Perhaps what we have endured will save our kids from making one of those irrevocable bad decisions. Maybe we can prevent even one heartache for our sons and daughters because of what we have been through. I often pray my kids can learn from my mistakes and have greater wisdom and discernment for the challenges they will face.

Having the right perspective on this issue can be so hard. Yes, our mistakes bring us hard-earned wisdom and experience. They also bring pain and regret that can haunt us even years after the fact.

When I struggle to find the balance, I lean on the Lord. I trust him. He knows what I need in order to heal, and he knows what my boys need to learn from my mistakes. He allowed me the free will to wander from him and make some horrible decisions. But more important, he gives me the grace and forgiveness to learn and move forward. He has granted me wisdom, and that's one treasure I want to pass on to my precious boys.

Our experiences, even the painful ones, shape who we are. And because of God's unconditional love and grace, he brings us through those experiences so we can support and instruct our kids.

It's difficult to be thankful in the middle of a crisis. But I try to look beyond the pain to see what God can teach me. And I try to remind myself that one day, I will have a clearer perspective on every trial. So I resolve to focus less on the pain and more on the invaluable wisdom I can pass on to Caedmen and Eli.

> *Lord,*
>
> *I pray right now for my children. I pray that my boys will desire to walk with you and strive for wisdom and discernment. I pray that I will not shy away from using what has happened in my past as cautionary tales. I want to be open and honest with my sons. My hope is that they will know you and love you. I ask that you will protect them as they journey through this life and face so may tough decisions. I pray that they truly will have a heart at rest in every situation.*
>
> *Thank you, Lord!*
>
> *Amen.*

5

Move Forward

Brothers and sisters, I do not consider myself yet to have
taken hold of it. But one thing I do: Forgetting what is
behind and straining toward what is ahead, I press on
toward the goal to win the prize for which God has called
me heavenward in Christ Jesus.
Philippians 3:13-14

I am blessed to live near Steamboat Springs, Colorado. Every day
I enjoy the beautiful mountains. A couple of days ago, I was trek-
king through the mountains with my favorite hiking partner—
my Siberian husky, Keva. We were enjoying one of our favorite
trails. The sun was shining, making the snow sparkle with millions
of tiny prisms. It was like God had sprinkled the landscape with
iridescent glitter. I was marveling in the beauty—and thanking
God for allowing me and my boys to live in such a place.

As we continued to hike, my spirits sank a bit. I told the Lord
I was discouraged despite the beauty of my surroundings. I felt
stuck in my life's journey, not moving much in any direction. I
knew I needed renewal, refreshment. I confessed that I needed
to be more thankful and to look to my Savior for direction, especially at a time like this. "I need a word from you," I prayed.

Suddenly, I looked up and was amazed at what I saw before
me. The words "Move Forward" were carved into a snowbank

near the trail. My first reaction was laughter. I wondered what led some random person to write those words in the snow. But then I thought a bit more—about my life and my recent prayer. "Wow!" I said. "Thank you, Lord."

I thought about what I needed to do to move forward, to get unstuck from the place I had been for too long. I sensed the Lord telling me to take one step, even if it was small. *You have to start somewhere,* I realized. *Why not here? One step will turn into two, and you will feel the progress of moving forward.*

I was reminded that each day is a fresh start, a fresh opportunity to move forward into what God has planned for me, into my destiny.

Now I am the one writing "Move Forward" in the snow, on the sidewalk (with chalk), and even in the mud. I hope those words will speak to someone just as they spoke to me that day in the mountains.

In John chapter 5, Jesus speaks to a man who has been an invalid for 38 years. "Do you want to get well?" Jesus asks. It's an amazing question in many ways. Of course the man wants to be healed. He has been disabled for decades. At first, he must have been dumbfounded by the question.

But I believe Jesus was looking at the man's heart and asking a much deeper question, the same kind of question he asks us today: "Do you truly want to move forward in your life? Do you want to be free of the burdens that are weighing you down?"

Jesus understands we can become comfortable in our misery. We would rather stay in a bad place than risk moving forward into the unknown. It's scary to venture into new territory.

Eventually, Jesus issues a direct command to the ailing man: "Get up! Pick up your mat and walk."

Each of us must decide how we will respond to this command. We must be honest with ourselves. Do we truly want to change our situation? Do we really want to get well?

If so, we need to gather the courage to take the first step.

I hope you will join me in that step.

Let's move forward.

> *Lord,*
>
> *So many times I stay stuck—even though that is not how I want to be, even though I complain about being stuck in the first place!*
>
> *And yet you are so gracious to all of us. You love us. You ask us, just as you asked the man in Scripture, "Do you want to get well?"*
>
> *Lord, my answer is yes! I thank you for allowing me to see those two key words, "Move Forward," written in the snow. I pray for strength to take those next steps in my life. Steps forward! That is where your destiny for me lies. So that's the direction I want to go.*
>
> *I pray we all will see the messages you have for us day by day. Open our eyes.*
>
> *In your precious and holy name,*
> *Amen.*

6

Living Water

All you thirsty ones, come to me! Come to me and drink!
Believe in me so that rivers of living water will burst out
from within you, flowing from your innermost being, just
like the Scripture says!

John 7:37-38 TPT

*W*ater is such a blessing to me! It is so alive with life. Here in Colorado, people gravitate to water with their lake houses, houseboats, kayaks, canoes, paddleboards, and more. They fish, camp, swim, snorkel, water-ski, and skip stones.

My son Caedmen got a kayak for his most recent birthday, and I just love to see him paddling around a lake. It brings him such calm, such joy, to be out there on the water. We recently went camping, and he took his kayak out for a sunset excursion. As the sun disappeared on the horizon, I saw his silhouette out in the distance on the still waters. I took a picture so I could capture that peaceful moment. Yes, there is just something about water.

Ironically, I am writing this devotion during fire season. This year's fires have been particularly devastating. Multiple blazes have broken out here in Colorado, and I know other states, including California and Oregon, are experiencing similar trials. It's terrible, the way fire consumes so much. It scorches the life out of our forests, often leaving behind nothing but ashes.

Right now, many people are praying for rain—physical rain and spiritual rain, with its renewing blessings. I find myself drawn to Isaiah 44:3-4:

> I will pour water on the thirsty land,
>   and streams on the dry ground;
> I will pour out my Spirit on your offspring,
>   and my blessing on your descendants.
> They will spring up like grass in a meadow,
>   like poplar trees by flowing streams.

A few years ago, I traveled to Uganda on a short-term mission. While there, I was amazed to see people from miles around travel from their villages to a water pump so they could fill their jugs with water. Then they carried those heavy jugs all the way back to their homes—on their heads!

Water is such a necessity, and I realized how those of us in industrialized nations can take its purity, accessibility, and relatively low cost for granted. In many parts of Africa, clean water is scarce and hard to obtain. It is treated as something very precious.

I was humbled and grateful when I left dry and desolate Africa for my home in Colorado, a "promised land" full of rivers and abundant vegetation.

Fortunately, all of us have ready access to the living waters that flow directly from God to us through the Holy Spirit. It is a joy to share this spiritual water with those close to us, especially our children. When they are spiritually thirsty, we can lead them to a well that will never run dry.

Thank you, Jesus, for your living water!

Heavenly Father,
Please send us rain! In the physical and spiritual
sense, we need what only you can provide. Keep our
eyes open and keep us looking to the skies for your
miraculous provision. Let us never forget that every
good thing comes from you!
In your precious name, our provider,
Amen.

7

Living On Purpose

*I run straight to the goal with purpose in every step. I fight
to win. I'm not just shadow-boxing or playing around.*
1 Corinthians 9:26 TLB

What is your passion in life? What do you enjoy more than anything else in the world—something you know you will never grow tired of? Maybe it's music, art, teaching others, or creative writing. If you have found your passion, you know there is a sense of wonder about it.

Dave Dravecky is a former Major League Baseball pitcher who now runs a ministry here in Colorado with his wife, Jan. It's called Endurance, and it provides spiritual support for people who are suffering, particularly cancer victims and amputees.

As a player, Dave loved his sport so much that he confessed, "I would have played for nothin'." Today, this cancer survivor and amputee brings that same kind of passion to his calling as a writer, speaker, and ministry leader.

What about you and me? Are we pursuing our passions? Are we fulfilling our highest purposes? Sure, there are required duties at home, on the job, or at school. We single moms are often doing double duty! But what about the world beyond the must-dos? Are you participating in the activities and pursuits you truly love or just the ones you think will lead to a better reputation, bank account, or résumé? What are you doing to ignite your sense of wonder and challenge yourself? In other words, are you making the grade or making a *difference*? Are you following the crowd or following the call of your heart?

Several years ago, I read an intriguing study of college students, comparing those who truly enjoyed their academic experience (and their lives in general) with those who were uncomfortable and unhappy with their place in life. The major difference between the two groups was that the former, by almost a two-to-one margin, felt a sense of underlying *purpose* about their lives—an advantage that was missing from their less-happy peers.[1]

So, if much of your life is sheer drudgery, you might be missing your life's ultimate purpose. Think about it: If you took away the paycheck, would you still want to do the job you have now? Would you "play for nothin'?"

You deserve no less than the best for your life. You deserve to experience a vibrant life, in perfect harmony with the abilities and passions God has given you. So don't let your life be a series of random events. Live it on purpose; live it with passion. You'll be happy you did.

True happiness is knowing you are constantly in the process of becoming what you were meant to be.

Dear Father,
I confess I don't always like being a single parent,
but I do love it. I know that it all matters—the
work I do at home as a parent and the work I do

elsewhere to provide for my family. How could any-thing be more meaningful than that? Thank you for this sacred privilege.

Amen.

8

Putting Disappointment in Its Place

Encourage one another daily, as long as it is called
"Today," so that none of you may be hardened by sin's
deceitfulness.

Hebrews 3:13

What do you do with the inevitable disappointments life hands you? Many people internalize them and let them creep into their hearts, where they fester and cause worry, pain, and despair.

Others are wiser, sharing disappointments with friends and relatives—or a pastor, counselor, or psychologist. People like these can be great sounding boards as well as great resources for solutions to problems.

As a single mom, do you make a habit of taking your disappointments to someone who cares about you? Do you pray to your heavenly Father? Let this approach be your first defense, not your last resort.

Maybe you hesitate to share your disappointments with others. You might think, "I feel guilty about complaining about my stupid problems in the face of all the important other stuff [the other person] is dealing with."

If you feel this way, give someone a chance. Your friend just might surprise you with how much he or she cares about even the little things. Your sibling might astonish you with her helpful insights. That counselor your coworker has been recommending might be even better than advertised.

Think about the great parents you know. Don't they care about their children's minor bumps and bruises and small problems as well as the major injuries and serious life difficulties? Would they want their kids to hide their small struggles and keep them to themselves? Of course not.

In a similar vein, does a good family doctor want to be aware of his or her patients' minor health problems as well as the biggies? In fact, catching health challenges when they are small can prevent them from growing into something more serious.

Every burden is lighter when you let someone share it. This is so important for us single parents to remember. And it's important to teach our children.

Dear God,
Thank you for the human lifelines you have placed in my life. Help me to overcome my fear of or hesitancy to reach out to them. After all, that's why we have family, friends, pastors, and professional counselors in the first place. Most of all, thank you for always being there for me.

In your loving name,
Amen.

9

Everyone's a Critic

A cheerful heart is good medicine,
but a crushed spirit dries up the bones.
Proverbs 17:22

*T*he other day I was at the grocery store, scrambling to find what I needed for that night's dinner. As I passed by the magazine display, I felt as if every periodical was attacking me. The gist of the messages: "10 Fatal Mistakes Parents Make—and You're Probably Making *Right Now*! (This Means You, Becky!)"

Where do you go when you struggle with feelings of inadequacy, like the ones I felt that day? Well, not to social media, that's for sure. Between the people boasting and posting about their supposedly perfect lives and the people ready to criticize our every action or word or photo, there's not much affirmation to be found. It seems that everyone's a critic. Sometimes I want to nickname my go-to social-media sites "Losing-Face Book" and "Insta-Slam."

So I was having a very discouraging shopping experience that day—until I recalled this story.

The famous British leader Winston Churchill had just finished a rousing speech. Upon his final words, the crowd who had gathered to hear him erupted with a thunderous ovation. However, when the clapping and cheering ceased, one man, unimpressed by Sir Winston's rhetoric, blew him "the raspberry."

The rest of the audience froze in suspense, awaiting the powerful statesman's response to the rude critic. Would he scream at the man and publicly humiliate him? Would he have him thrown out of the place? Churchill looked at his tormentor and then spoke. "I know," he said good-naturedly. "I agree with you. But what are we among so many?"

Churchill's humble and humorous reply was a hit with the throng, and the tense situation was quickly diffused.

Like Sir Winston, you might occasionally face insults or criticism from a jealous or mean-spirited nemesis. It might be from your ex, or your ex's family, or even a well-meaning person from church. In such cases, you might be tempted to become angry and lose your composure. And in today's power-is-everything world, conventional wisdom tells people to be defiant in the face of criticism, to fight fire with fire. Unfortunately, this approach usually leads to someone getting burned.

Don't forget the power of humility and humor to relax a tense situation. As King Solomon pointed out centuries ago, "A gentle answer will calm a person's anger, but an unkind answer will cause more anger" (Proverbs 15:1 NCV).

Certainly, there will be times when you must forcefully defend yourself, or your kids, or a friend. Be watchful, however, for those times when a clever, self-deprecating comeback can disarm even the most hostile of foes, the harshest of internet critics.

Remember, if God has provided basic health, the love of friends and family, and some food and shelter, we are rich—rich enough be able to afford some jokes at our own expense.

Heavenly Father,
Criticism abounds in modern life. I must admit
that it really hurts sometimes. Help me to trust that
the people who truly care about me aren't looking
for reasons to criticize. And help me to remember
that ultimately, I am trying to please an audience
of One. Let me hear your voice above all the others.
                              In your life-giving name,
                                              Amen.

10

Savoring Life's Flavors

Sing to the LORD a new song;
sing to the LORD, all the earth.
Sing to the LORD, praise his name;
proclaim his salvation day after day.

Psalm 96:1-2

*M*agic moments. You've had them. Chugging a bubbling soda after a hot day of outdoor work. Standing and cheering at the end of an inspiring song at a concert. Holding a little child's hand on a walk to the park or ice cream shop. Seeing that familiar smile burst across your best friend's face when you unexpectedly bump into each other at the coffee shop. Having a relative mention *your* name when thanking God for life's blessings during a pre-meal prayer.

Every good and perfect moment like this is a gift. Every one—even the ones that seem like happenstance or coincidence. God has a way of sending these gifts to remind us there is more good in the world than bad. God offers a supply of love and kindness that will never run dry. And because of this, life is always worth living. What a wonderful truth for us to remember and to share with our kids.

These gifts also remind us to keep our eyes, minds, and hearts open for the blessings, large and small, that await us in the future. Instead of dreading all that *might* go wrong tomorrow, next month, or next year, happy people spend their energy being watchful for those magic moments, the ones that fill our mouths with laughter and make us want to shout with joy.

So the next time life drops one of these blessings on your tongue, take time to savor it, to enjoy it. A seemingly momentary blessing can leave a sweet aftertaste that can last forever, so let it.

Your heavenly Father will load your world with gifts, large and small. Take the time to open them all!

> *Dear God,*
> *Single motherhood is full of challenges, but it is full of blessings too. Help me to remember that true happiness is not a status we eventually attain. It's not a destination, but rather a manner of traveling. Help my kids and me to live joyfully in the knowledge that many small-but-happy moments add up to a life well lived.*
> *Thank you for blessings large and small!*
> *Amen.*

11

Set the Right Kind of Goals

I strive always to keep my conscience clear
before God and man.
Acts 24:16

I know two guys named Thomas and Steve. They graduated the same year from the same college. Throughout their undergraduate experience, they compared report cards, girlfriends, job prospects, and fantasy football successes and failures.

Steve usually came out on top in the various competitions, but Thomas resolved that he would beat his nemesis when school was over and "real life" began. After college, Steve landed a high-paying job at a high-tech firm. Thomas, a journalism major, earned job offers from a few small newspapers but turned them down because he didn't like the salaries. They were about half what Steve was making.

A few months later, Thomas signed on with an advertising agency. The money was good, but the hours were long and the stress levels in the office were perpetually at the boiling point. Most evenings, Thomas returned to his apartment exhausted and frustrated. Some nights, he didn't come home at all, falling asleep at his workspace after a 16-hour day. *At least I'm keeping up with Steve*, he told himself.

About a year later, Steve called Thomas. "I guess you win, dude," he muttered. "I just got downsized."

Thomas offered his sympathies and then hung up the phone. He thought he would feel victorious, but what he really felt was empty. He took no joy in climbing past his old buddy on the career ladder. His life wasn't made one bit better because of Steve's misfortune. He realized that for years, he had been competing in a game he didn't really want to win. (He wasn't sure if he even wanted to *compete*.) He was making lots of money in a job he hated, in a business he had no passion for.

The next day, Steve began a search for a newspaper job, the kind he had really wanted for a long time. He ended up taking a 40 percent pay cut, but in the exchange he found a job he looked forward to each day.

Pursuing the right kind of goals is critical to a person's life satisfaction. If your life goals match your self-concept and your values, it will increase by a whopping 43 percent the likelihood that your career pursuits will enhance your level of satisfaction with life.[2]

I don't know any single moms (or single dads) who don't struggle when it comes to job choices and career development. Sometimes we get an opportunity that would launch us forward on our career path, but it might adversely affect our kids. So many choices. So many *difficult* choices. I live in an area that doesn't abound with job opportunities. But I do live in a beautiful place with good schools and a grace-filled church. My boys and I have great friends here. I could probably move to another city and make more money, but how do you put a price tag on the peace of mind and well-being of your family?

This brings us back to goals. We should always be asking ourselves, *What are the most important goals for me right now?* We must be honest with ourselves about this. We should focus on what truly matters to us—not on what will make us look good on social media or give us bragging rights at the next high school or college reunion.

If you are struggling with job-related decisions, I encourage you to talk with your kids. Not to put the pressure of a decision on them, but to explore their needs, wants, and opinions. Beyond this, seek wise and godly counsel anywhere you can find it.

The Bible assures us that where our treasure is, there our hearts will be. Let's prayerfully examine what truly matters to us and live accordingly. Remember, it is not the size of our treasure that matters; it's whether our treasure represents who we truly are.

> *Wise Father,*
> *I thank you for the abilities you have given me. Please show me how to use them most wisely. I want to contribute something good to my community—and to the world if I can. More important, thank you for my spiritual gifts. May I value these blessings more than anything in the material world. As I strive to provide for my family, help me order or reorder my priorities. If that means giving up money or status, so be it. I ask you for the wisdom to make the right choices—and the courage to act on them.*
>
> *In your name,*
> *Amen.*

12

Picking Our Battles

"In your anger do not sin":
Do not let the sun go down while you are still angry,
and do not give the devil a foothold.
Ephesians 4:26-27

I know this guy whom I will call Jason. He and his boss, Tammy, seemed to be in a constant state of conflict. They found themselves arguing about almost everything—from Jason's job performance to the department's mission statement to their differing communication styles. Regardless of the subject, their unfortunate chemistry almost always resulted in an explosion.

Avoiding conflict and reprimands from his supervisor became Jason's constant quest. He dreaded every meeting, especially his weekly one-on-ones with Tammy. To avoid unpleasant confrontations, Jason tried to use email for most of his communication, but the result was often an endless back-and-forth of tersely worded accusations, insinuations, and justifications.

Jason felt like the mythological Sisyphus, who was doomed to spend his life pushing a boulder up a hill. Every time Sisyphus got close to the top, he found himself unable to move the rock against the steep grade. He would lose his hold, and the boulder would roll back down to the bottom. He was imprisoned by a task that had no point and no solution.

After two years in a miserable work situation, Jason decided he didn't want to spend his career like a tragic mythological figure. He realized that Tammy held all the power on the job and that he wasn't going to "win" his struggle with her, no matter how much passion or research he brought to the battle. They simply clashed.

Jason visited his company's HR department and eventually secured a transfer to another division in the company with a new manager. His job satisfaction skyrocketed almost immediately.

"I didn't fully realize how fighting a losing battle every day was destroying me," he said later. "And to be fair, I'm sure it was no picnic for my former boss either."

As a single mom, I found that this story impacted me significantly. We face challenges with our exes, their families, their friends, and so on. It can be deceptively easy to get drawn into a conflict with no real point. A conflict in which, even if you "win," you actually lose.

Of course, sometimes there are issues that must be dealt with. But I wonder how many times divorced parents stop to ask themselves, *Is the outcome of this "discussion" worth the effort, or are my ex and I fighting just because that's what we tend to do?*

On a similar theme, we should be careful about conflicts with our kids. Of course, if there is a discipline issue, we must deal with it. But how many times do we find ourselves yelling or crying about something trivial simply because we are tired, stressed, or overwhelmed?

Dwelling on unwinnable battles wastes our time and drains our morale. Life is too short to devote energy to something you cannot change...or don't really *need* to change. So don't keep fighting the same pointless battle over and over. Try to arrive at a truce. Or better yet, move on. Your brain, your stomach lining, and your friends and family will be glad you did.

> *"Conflict is inevitable, but combat is optional."*
> —Max Lucado

13

Every Child Is a Child of God

We are God's handiwork, created in Christ Jesus to do
good works, which God prepared in advance for us to do.
Ephesians 2:10

When it comes to addressing difficult questions with my boys,
I enjoy presenting a real-life scenario to them and then having a
conversation about it. Here is an example.

A medical school professor once posed this bioethics question
to a group of students:

> Here's a family history. The father is an abusive alco-
> holic and may have syphilis. The mother has TB,
> which will eventually prove fatal. She has given birth to
> two sons, neither of whom survived infancy. Now the
> mother is pregnant again. The parents are despondent
> and come to you for advice. They are unsure how to
> care for a child that may have serious health problems.
> They are unsure if they should carry the pregnancy to
> term, and they say they need to take steps to ensure
> they have no more children.

The students shared their various opinions in a lively discussion. Some chastised the parents for allowing another pregnancy.

Some said this pregnancy should be terminated, as they doubted the parents' ability to care properly for a child. Others suggested that if the newborn does in fact have developmental challenges, the parents should plan on placing him or her in an institution soon after birth. Although their solutions varied, none of the class members held much hope for the unborn child.

That's when the professor did his big reveal. "Before we go any further with this discussion," he said, "I probably should note that this story is real. The child is Ludwig von Beethoven."

The lesson here? A person's inherent value and potential don't depend on family background or social status or even likelihood of success in life. Every person on the planet possesses worth and skill and promise. The way you treat those around you shouldn't be tainted by a prejudice based on race, religion, economic status, physical appearance, or disability. This advice might seem like a no-brainer, but many people are shocked when they honestly evaluate the way they perceive and treat others.

I know that single moms can feel a sense of inadequacy—that our kids are beginning an important race from miles behind the start line. At times like these, I draw strength from stories like Beethoven's. And from the long legacy of successful people raised by single moms, from entertainers like Kate Beckinsale, Barbra Streisand, and Pierce Brosnan to athletes like Julia Mancuso, Jackie Robinson, Shaquille O'Neal, and LeBron James. Even a few of our US presidents were parented by single moms.

Like Beethoven (and LeBron!), every person has potential to add music to the great symphony of life. That includes the people you encounter every day, and your kids, and you too.

You and everyone around you have way more potential than you have history or heritage. And that's something to be happy about.

> *Heavenly Father,*
> *I thank you for giving me life. Thank you for the life of my kids. I am freshly amazed every time I contemplate the fact that you know us by name. We are so grateful to be part of your family. Please keep our eyes focused on you. Our ultimate worth comes from you. We are precious in your sight, and that is a truth we will always hold precious.*
>
> *Amen.*

14

Together Is Better

Though one may be overpowered,
two can defend themselves.
A cord of three strands is not quickly broken.
Ecclesiastes 4:12-13

*A*s I try to teach my two boys good life principles, I often find myself turning to God's creation. For example, we can learn a lot about teamwork from the emperor penguins of Antarctica. These beautiful (and endangered) creatures huddle together by the thousands, sharing warmth that allows them to survive the brutal, freezing weather—temperatures that can make a steel screwdriver as brittle as a pretzel.

The penguins take turns monitoring the outside of their giant huddle, on the lookout for danger or food. After one of the birds has finished its perimeter duty, it moves to the inside of the group so it can get warm and sleep. The baby penguins stand on their moms' and dads' feet to protect themselves from the icy surface. If a penguin tried to survive alone, it wouldn't make it through one frozen winter night.

We can all learn from these penguins. Teamwork can equal survival. And the tougher the conditions, the more important it is for people to band together. You may never need to share physical warmth—unless your school, home, or office heater goes out this winter—but you can share encouragement, joy, empathy, and ideas.

You can share the workload on a huge project or join a study group before finals. And there's something else you can share—the sense of success and accomplishment that result from committed, unselfish teamwork. As single moms, we are working with teams that are not as large as they used to be, but smaller doesn't mean weaker or less committed to one another.

Wise King Solomon noted that "a cord of three strands is not quickly broken." Imagine how strong a cord of five, ten, or fifty of you and your friends and family can be. And imagine the fun you can have tackling life's tasks, challenges, and problems *together.*

> *"Find a group of people who challenge and*
> *inspire you. Spend a lot of time with them,*
> *and it will change your life forever."*
>
> —Amy Poehler

15

Playing Life by Ear

Love from the center of who you are; don't fake it...
Be good friends who love deeply;
practice playing second fiddle.
Romans 12:9-10 MSG

Want to do something kind and meaningful for the people in your life? Especially for the kid or kids in your life? Listen to them. Really listen. Women are traditionally known as better listeners than men (and in this case, tradition is right...just sayin'), but even we can fall into the mode of robotically nodding our heads and muttering "Uh-huh" as we go about our tasks or wait for our turn to talk. Truly listening means thinking about the words being said, the tone of voice, and the body language that accompanies those words.

People today are bombarded with messages. Voices ring out everywhere. Everyone talks. Few truly listen. Whether it's your friends, neighbors, relatives, or yes, even your ex-husband or new boyfriend, your willingness to listen to them can be one of the greatest gifts you can give. It's a profound way to show you truly care.

Want an example? In the 1800s, two powerful men vied for political leadership of Great Britain. Both men, William Gladstone and Benjamin Disraeli, were intelligent, successful, and important. However, Disraeli had a distinct advantage that was best expressed by a thoughtful woman who happened to dine with the two statesmen on consecutive evenings.

Her assessment of Gladstone: "When I left the dining room after sitting next to Mister Gladstone, I thought he was the cleverest man in England."

Following her dinner with Disraeli, however, she said, "After sitting next to Mister Disraeli, I thought *I* was the cleverest woman in England!"

Many people today are obsessed with proving how clever and important they are. You can stand apart from the crowd and make a difference in the lives of those around you by abstaining from all the self-promotion and lending an ear (better yet, two ears) to make others feel valued and important.

As Disraeli himself understood, "The greatest good you can do for others is not just to share your riches, but to reveal to them their own."

Attentive heavenly Father,
I know your Word instructs us to be quick to listen and slow to speak, but we often get it backward. Help me show the people in my life, especially my kids, that I value them by the way I listen to them.
Thank you for listening to my prayers!
Amen.

16

Tuning In to the God Channel

The LORD God then said:
I will look for my sheep and take care of them myself.
Ezekiel 34:11 CEV

The God of the entire universe longs to communicate with *you*! Let that truth sink in for a moment. It's amazing but true.

Many of us would consider it the opportunity of a lifetime just to talk with a favorite recording artist, athlete, CEO, or movie star—even just once! We would be eager to tell our girlfriends or our kids about our "brush with greatness," knowing they would be impressed (and probably jealous).

Unfortunately, we don't always show the same zeal for communicating with God, who loves us, who is far more fascinating than any person we could ever encounter, and who longs to fellowship with us.

God created the universe and everything in it—including the big shots we revere. He created us to have a relationship with him. And the only way to have a relationship with anyone is to spend time with him or her. With God, this time can include prayer, meditation, reading the Bible or Christian books, listening to music, and worship.

Think about it. What relationship is more important than your personal relationship with God? Who is more worth knowing? After all, God created you, he loves you, and he has all the answers. What's more, your bond with him forms the foundation for all other relationships.

The Lord of all creation is waiting for you. You might not know him well, but he knows you. He wants to hear from you. There is no risk. God will never betray your relationship with him. So don't wait another second. Open your eyes; open your heart. God wants to communicate with you right now!

Remember, even if you have neglected your relationship with God, he still yearns to be close to you. He holds no grudges. Instead, he holds his people close at heart.

Dear God,
I marvel that you want to communicate with me.
Forgive me for the times I have failed to appreciate
this sacred privilege. Life is all about relationships,
and I know my relationship with you sets the tone
for all the others.

In your name,
Amen.

17

Spiritual Ears

Faith comes from hearing the message, and the
message is heard through the word about Christ.
Romans 10:17

I read this verse a few days ago, and it sparked me to think about the way God speaks to his children. He doesn't shout at us. Instead, he often whispers because that's the best way to teach us how to listen, how to truly hear him. He uses that still, small voice. The kind of voice that speaks to your heart more than your head.

God doesn't need to shout at me, because he's in my heart. I hope he is in your heart too. This closeness allows God to speak *in* us, not just *to* us. There is something more personal about a voice that comes from within. Even when it's quiet, it penetrates directly to our hearts, something all that outside noise simply cannot do.

When I think of how my heavenly Father speaks to me, it makes me love him even more. As I talk with friends and family, I realize how many had a loud, domineering father or spouse. They felt shouted at, scolded, and demeaned. Today, they remember the escalating volume of those times, and they struggle to even imagine a God who can speak in a whisper. A God who is gentle even when he is correcting us. What a wonderful example of how we should speak to our children.

I wonder if you are like me. When I am being berated, I shut down. I stop listening. My boys are the same way. If you want them to respond, you must speak with a calm and loving voice. When this happens, they respond with open ears and open hearts.

Of course, it's not always easy to listen, no matter how young or how old we are. I confess that there are times Caedmen and Eli are telling me stories of their latest video game victories or about the new YouTube channel they are enjoying, and I catch myself not fully listening. I mumble "Uh-huh" and hope they don't note my lack of interest.

Writing this book has helped me appreciate their enthusiasm and their eagerness to share it with me. I want to give them my full attention, so I am disciplining myself to tell the person on the other end of the phone, "Hey, let me call you back; one of my kids needs me." Sometimes you need to set aside the smartphone or the spatula and look a kid in the eyes.

When my kids get home from school, they always have things they want to share with me. I want to be present for them. I know that a day might come when they don't want to talk with me. They might get home from school and head straight for their rooms. So I want to make time now. I want to keep the lines of communication open for my kids, just as the Lord does for me.

I want my spiritual ears to be open. I want to hear God's voice, even his softest whisper. I want to put away all distractions and focus on him. The Scriptures assure us that faith comes by hearing, and hearing comes from the word about Christ. I know my faith will grow as I listen to my heavenly Father and carve out time to spend in the Bible. I want to be like the sheep Jesus describes in John 10:4: "When he has brought out all his sheep, he walks ahead of them and they will follow him, for they are familiar with his voice" (TPT).

> *Heavenly Father,*
> *I pray that you will open my spiritual ears so I will be able to hear your voice—even your quiet whisper. I pray that you will give me that calmness and that quiet voice when it comes to my children. I pray that my faith will increase as I study your Word and listen for your voice. As the sheep knew the shepherd's voice, I pray that I will know your voice, that I can be an example to my children of what it means to walk with you to hear your voice.*
>
> *Thank you, Lord. In your precious name,*
> *Amen.*

18

I Chose You

God raised us up with Christ and seated us with him in
the heavenly realms in Christ Jesus, in order that in the
coming ages he might show the incomparable riches of
his grace, expressed in his kindness to us in Christ Jesus.

Ephesians 2:6-7

*F*or anyone with a conscience, guilt comes with the territory. Single moms, single dads...we all feel guilty. We all feel shame. And a certain amount of guilt isn't necessarily a bad thing. We should feel bad when we hurt another person or behave in a way that's inconsistent with our moral code. But guilt can be destructive when it covers us like a dark cloud day after day or year after year.

If it goes unchecked, guilt can take over our thoughts and emotions, leaving us with a feeling of worthlessness.

God wants us to acknowledge our shortcomings when we miss the mark, but he doesn't want us to live our lives covered in a shroud of shame. He wants us to be able to say, "I am forgiven, and I am going to learn from my mistakes. I'm not going to walk in shame anymore!"

I fail as a mom plenty of times. I lose it. I know many essential parenting techniques, but I don't practice them consistently. I need to say it one more time: As a parent, I fail again and again.

As I talk with my friends, I see that I am not alone. Who

among us can get through a day without at least one parental mistake? This can be frustrating. I tend to beat myself up when I fall short, and I fail to reach out for God's grace.

One of my life's priorities right now is seeking that place of grace. I would love to lay my head on my pillow at night and think, *I am worthy. I am not going to let guilt and shame overshadow me anymore. I am forgiven.*

I pray that God will wash away my guilt so I can be emotionally and spiritually healthier for my two boys. I don't want guilt to steal my joy.

Romans 3:23, a verse you might know by heart, states that we all fall short of God's glory. That's a given. But what is amazing is that Jesus's blood washes us whiter than snow, whiter than the freshest snow on the highest mountaintop here in Colorado.

Jesus wants us to ask for forgiveness, not so he can shame us, but so we can repent and return to living the way we should. God wants us to truly live. And he wants us to know for certain that we are his.

This is such a vital realization because we can't change the past. We must accept God's forgiveness, forgive ourselves, let go of the past, and move forward. We can find hope in striving to do better next time. This is what I am trying to do right now—focus on what I can do better day by day and even moment by moment. Even the small steps forward matter.

A few Sundays ago, I was able to hear my precious dad preach. Here's my key takeaway from that sermon: To be a good mother or a good father, we must learn to become a good son or good daughter of our heavenly Father.

In John 14:6-7, Jesus says, "I am the way and the truth and the life. No one comes to the Father except through me. If you really know me, you will know my Father as well. From now on, you do know him and have seen him."

To know Jesus is to know the Father. We are his children—sons and daughters with a precious inheritance. We can share this amazing truth with our children: We are covered by grace. We are covered *in* grace.

> *Heavenly Father,*
> *Thank you, Lord, that when we fail, you cover us in Jesus's blood. Your grace inspires me to do better the next time. In your Word, you assure us that you chose us. I pray that we can live this life knowing that we are yours. We are children of God.*
>
> *Please teach me how to be a good daughter to you so I can be a good mother to my children.*
> *In your precious name,*
> *Amen.*

19

National _____ Day!

> They ate and drank with great joy in the presence of the
> LORD that day.
> 1 Chronicles 29:22

*D*uring all my parenting years, I have strived to create special moments of joy to share with my boys. I know they won't forget making these memories with their mom. When I became a single mom, I put extra effort into making the most of difficult, emotionally messy days—times when we felt alone and I could tell that my boys were missing their dad. I know the Lord gave these special times, and I don't regret the costs, monetary and otherwise, that I invested in creating these memories.

I drew inspiration from my friend Chrissy. She did in-home childcare for a few children while their parents worked. I always cracked up when I stopped by for a visit. Her house looked like a bomb had exploded inside, and that's not much of an exaggeration. I would see flour coating the kitchen floor and the chairs as she and her little helpers created homemade pizza. Their messy faces broke into huge grins as they molded the dough into imperfectly shaped "circles."

A child didn't have to be a babysitting client to join the fun. Chrissy's doors were (literally) wide open to anyone who wanted to pop in and help with the day's culinary creation. While Chrissy and the kids did their thing, her huge Great Pyrenees, Gussie, would wander in and out of the house. (That dog could not get enough of me. He loved me, and boy, do I miss him now that he's no longer around.)

With Chrissy, the adventures were not limited to the kitchen. I remember seeing muddy handprints everywhere. I saw kids holding garter snakes, salamanders, sow bugs, roly-poly bugs, ladybugs, butterflies, and various other critters.

When the kids tired of the great indoors, they headed for Chrissy's garden, which was the best in the neighborhood. There she put her many little helpers to work. They made more messes, but they learned about gardening in the process.

She once made a teepee out of sticks, and soon, vines of sugar snap peas and sweet peas were climbing to the top.

The garden also featured rows and rows of kale, Swiss chard, lettuce, strawberries, zucchini, and more. Chrissy never let me leave without picking a huge bag full of fresh greens.

In contrast to Chrissy, I tend to be self-conscious if someone pops in for a visit while my house is a horrible mess. But then I think of this dear friend and how she loved to make memories for her kids—and any kids who wanted to join in.

She wanted kids to get grubby and experience life in all its occasional messiness. The pizzas, the garden, the art projects—none of them were perfect. But they were perfect for those little ones.

Eventually, Chrissy inspired me. I decided I would lean in to whatever National _____ Day popped up on the calendar. National Pizza Day, National Ice Cream Day, National Inventors

Day, National Spaghetti Day, National Extraterrestrial Abduction Day...I was up for almost anything.

Late one Friday (June 7, to be exact), I finally got around to looking up the appropriate reason to celebrate that day. I saw that it was National Donut Day. So despite the late hour, I determined I would create homemade donuts with my boys. If you've ever made donuts this way, you know it's a complete mess, even under the best circumstances.

And because the dough must rise, it's also a lengthy process. I think it was past ten before the donuts, coated in sticky but yummy glaze, were ready to eat. We had a blast, but I think I created two National (Whatever) Day monsters in the process. I don't need to look up special occasions on the internet anymore. I have two consultants who tell me regularly what day it is—especially if that day celebrates something messy.

If the day is silly and fun, we are all over it.

Of course, we don't need a specific day to celebrate. When autumn rolls around, we love to turn off the lights, blast *Thriller* throughout the house, and do some Michael Jackson–style dancing. Sometimes, people drop by for a visit and question our sanity. That's okay with me.

You see, there is always quite enough sadness, stress, and worry in life. So if I can create some fun little memories with my kids, it's worth the effort—and the strange looks we might receive. It's been a few years now since that inaugural National Donut Day celebration, but my boys still talk about it. I won't forget it either. I won't forget my friend Chrissy (and big Gussie) and how they inspired me.

In fact, I won't forget any of the fun and messy memories God has allowed me to create. They were perfect.

> *Father God,*
> *Thank you for the blessings around us. Thank you for the moments we can share with our children and the memories we can make. I am grateful that even though I am far from perfect, I can make perfectly messy times with my kids. Thank you for the people you have placed in my life who have showed me how to have fun and find more enjoyment in these days you have provided.*
>
> *During the week ahead, help me to find the time to make a memory with my kids. Let us do one more fun thing that none of us will ever forget.*
> *In your precious name,*
> *Amen.*

In case this devotion has left you feeling adventurous, here is my kid-tested donut recipe. National Donut Day is the first Friday in June, but you can do your own thing whenever you want. National Carbohydrates Day, perhaps?

Rebecca List-Bergeron's National Donut Day Donuts

Donut Ingredients

2 envelopes dry yeast

¼ cup warm water
(105 to 115 degrees)

½ cup lukewarm milk

½ cup white sugar

1 tsp. salt

2 eggs

⅓ cup shortening

5 cups all-purpose flour

1 quart vegetable oil (for frying)

Glaze Ingredients

⅓ cup butter

1½ cups confectioners' sugar, sifted
to remove any lumps

2 tsp. vanilla extract (optional but
recommended)

3 to 4 T. milk (hot water works too)

Directions

Sprinkle the yeast over the warm water. Let the mixture stand for 5 minutes or until foamy.

In a large bowl, combine the yeast/water mixture, milk, sugar, salt, eggs, shortening, and 2 cups of the flour. Mix for a few minutes on low speed. (If you prefer, you can stir with a wooden spoon.) Beat in the remaining flour, a half cup at a time, until the dough no longer sticks to the bowl. Knead for about 5 minutes or until the dough is smooth and elastic. Place the dough into a greased bowl and cover. Set in a warm place until the dough rises to double its original size. The dough is ready if you touch it and an indention remains.

Turn the dough out onto a floured surface and gently roll out to half-inch thickness. Cut with a floured doughnut cutter. Let doughnuts sit out to rise again until their size doubles. Cover loosely with a cloth.

To make icing for your donuts, melt butter in a saucepan over medium heat. Stir in confectioners' sugar and vanilla until smooth. Remove from heat and stir in hot water or milk one tablespoon at a time until the icing is somewhat thin but not too runny. Set aside.

Heat oil in a deep fryer or large heavy skillet to 350 degrees. Slide doughnuts into the hot oil using a wide spatula. Turn doughnuts over as they rise to the surface. Fry doughnuts on each side until golden brown. Remove from hot oil and drain on a wire rack. Dip doughnuts into the glaze while still hot. Place donuts on wire racks to drain off excess glaze. Keep a cookie sheet or tray (or parchment paper) under racks for easier cleanup.

Enjoy—and don't worry about the mess!

20

Uniquely Unique

Start children off on the way they should go,
and even when they are old they will not turn from it.
Proverbs 22:6

I am so thankful that I grew up in a godly home and that my mom and dad were such good role models to my sisters and me. In today's world, there are so many broken families, so many hurt feelings and offenses. I know families in which members haven't spoken to each other for years.

I know others who have completely severed relationships with family (or former family). There is no communication at all. As I have mentioned earlier in this book, my biological father and my mom divorced when I was very young. This could have caused long-term damage to my self-worth, but my mom remarried a wonderful man, and they gave me a godly upbringing that is important to me to this day.

I look at my two boys and am filled with love for them. I am doing my best to raise them the right way. I want them to know they are special, unique guys who are a vital part of our larger family. "Family" is a treasured word for me. I want my boys to know they can come to me with any challenge or problem. I want to be able to communicate openly and honestly with them as they continue to grow.

Sometimes people look at me, a person who grew up with only sisters, and wonder how I manage to single-parent two boys. But those people don't know me very well.

I grew up a very adventurous tomboy. I started walking at eight months. I learned to climb shortly after that. When I was only ten months old, my mom found me perched on top of our refrigerator. That was only a preview of the challenges I would present.

I spent an inordinate amount of my younger years in the pediatrician's office due to various accidents, several of which required stitches. It got to the point where the doctor would greet my mom by asking, "What did Becky get into *this* time?"

While girls my age were asking for Barbies and other dolls for Christmas and their birthdays, I preferred Transformers and toy trucks. I also loved race-car tracks and train sets. I would put everything together and play for hours.

My two sisters, one older and one younger, loved their Barbies. I showed no such affection. I enjoyed taking their dolls and squishing down their heads until those long, slender doll necks disappeared.

When I became a teenager, most of my friends had bedroom walls adorned with boy-band posters: New Kids on the Block, Backstreet Boys, and the like.

Not Becky. I favored posters of cars, especially Lamborghinis and Ferraris.

At the amusement park, I just had to ride the scariest ride. If others in our group were afraid of something, I was all in.

When I was outdoors, I sought out the largest rocks to

scramble up. Then I would leap from rock to rock. If someone cautioned me, I would respond with, "You only live once!"

Indoors, even family games like Tri-Ominos, Pictionary, and Uno became fierce competitions. I hated to lose. (I still do.) Today, my mom and dad like to tell my boys stories about just how competitive I was.

I remember playing capture the flag for hours with the neighborhood boys and striving to out-climb them on the neighborhood trees. I was a monkey.

When we lived in Oklahoma, I found a great way to torment my sisters. I would pick up "cow patties" and toss them like Frisbees at Vania and Rachel. I know this might sound gross, but I resolved not to be grossed out by anything. I wanted to be brave and to stand apart from the stereotypical "girlie girls."

Besides, seeing my sisters react to the dried cow waste flying their way? That was worth the unpleasantness of picking it up and throwing it.

I was not into anything glittery, sparkly, or pink. I had no use for cute shoes, beautiful purses, or makeup.

So yes, God knew exactly what he was doing when he gave me two boys. I have had the best time being Mom to my boys.

My sons are very close to one another—and very different from each other.

Caedmen, my older son, is an artist who loves exploring nature. He is quiet, a thinker. He loves to watch documentaries and learn about life. He will watch just about anything connected to outer space or the oceans. We love watching shows like *Shark* and *Monster Fish* together, along with just about anything on Animal Planet.

Caedmen is cautious. He definitely did not adopt my "You only live once!" philosophy. He says "no, thanks" to the bone-chilling rides at the amusement park, and I am just fine with that.

He is a bit shy, and it takes him a while to make new friends. But the friends he has are close. When he was in fourth grade, he was diagnosed with dyslexia. This makes certain school classes difficult, but he is a gifted artist, and that makes up for the areas that are challenging for him. He is a talented painter, and he can plan and build amazing LEGO creations.

I believe God will use Caedmen's artistic talents throughout his life. More important to me, he is a sweet and tender boy. His quiet nature and kindness are evident to everyone who encounters him.

Eli, my younger son, is busy, crazy, and always trying to make people laugh. He loves to compete and to try new things. When he was a baby, I turned my back to him for just a moment, and he somehow scrambled to the top of our metal spiral staircase, which was ten feet high. I saw him sitting up there and thought, *Oh boy, now I know what my mom went through with me when I was a baby!*

Eli has played soccer since he was five, but this fall he is trying football. I guess this is a good thing—since practice has started, he has spent less time trying to tackle his big brother.

He is well liked, and people seem to gravitate to him. He makes friends easily. At school, he excels without breaking a sweat. When we go to the amusement park, he is like me, seeking the most terrifying rides. I am usually the one who ends up riding with him, although I confess I am not as much of a daredevil as I used to be.

Like his big brother, Eli is a sweet boy. He loves it when a teacher asks him to help a classmate, even a "difficult" classmate. He has a lot of compassion for others.

When I look at my boys and consider their differences, I think of my sisters and me when we were growing up. We all have unique qualities, and I can see how God placed us in our respective families for a reason.

I don't want to paint an overly sweet picture here. As a single mom, I struggle at times. Occasionally, my boys simply don't want to listen to me. They complain about their chores. They complain about going to school. And sometimes they fight with each other. At times like these, I remind myself that my boys are in the Lord's hands. He is going to walk beside me as I raise them, every step of the way. And I recall something my mom was always saying during my childhood: "When you really don't want to do something, when the burden seems too heavy to carry, do it as unto the Lord. Tell yourself you are doing this chore to honor God." This really put things into perspective for me.

My mom's words reflect the wisdom of Colossians 3:23-35:

> Put your heart and soul into every activity you do, as though you are doing it for the Lord himself and not merely for others.
>
> For we know that we will receive a reward, an inheritance from the Lord, as we serve the Lord Yahweh, the Anointed One! A disciple will be repaid for what he has learned and followed, for God pays no attention to the titles or prestige of men (TPT).

I lean on Scriptures like this in times of challenge. And I remember the proverb that began this chapter. It's good to remind myself that my boys' lives are in God's hands. The values I strive to instill in them day after day will sustain them. And someday, Caedmen and Eli will pass these treasures on to their own children. Just as my parents did for me.

> *Heavenly Father,*
> *Thank you for blessing me by allowing me to be a mom to my kids. Thank you for the family I come from. I know you placed me there. Thank you for the lessons my family gave me.*
>
> *I turn my heart now to the broken families out there. I pray you will restore them. I pray you will soften the hardened hearts and provide a desire to reconcile, to forgive. I pray the people in these struggling families will see one another through your eyes, Lord.*
>
> *Finally, I pray that I will instill in my boys the values you want them to have. Let me always point them toward you. May I discover a new appreciation for all the unique qualities represented in my family, for we are all special and precious in your eyes.*
>
> *I love you, Lord. In your precious name,*
> *Amen.*

21

Bloom Where You Are Planted

I have told you these things, so that in me you may have
peace. In this world you will have trouble. But take heart! I
have overcome the world.

John 16:33

When I was growing up, my mom used little sayings to help me remember key truths about life. In fact, she still graces me with these words of wisdom. I am amazed at how many of these sayings have stuck with me.

As a child, I didn't always appreciate the wisdom at the time. But today, as a mom myself, I realize just how wise and practical those words are. One of my mom's favorites was, "Bloom where you are planted."

My mom was a great role model for this concept. She was born in Africa, literally on the mission field. At a very young age, she was sent to boarding school, far away from her mom and dad. Early in life, she learned the hard lessons of blooming in situations that were strange, uncomfortable, and sometimes even dangerous.

When I hear those words in my head, "Bloom where you are planted," I always envision a fragile little flower poking its head through a thin crack in a concrete sidewalk. That flower is surrounded by a hard environment, much like my mom was. Yet somehow that flower is finding a way to stretch, to reach up for the sun and bloom!

Today, I deliver the same message to my boys. I want to teach them that no matter the season in life, no matter the circumstances, they can learn, grow, and reach up to the Son. I want Caedmen and Eli to know that if Jesus is growing in their lives, he will touch and bless other people through them.

> *"Find the good. It's all around you. Find it,
> showcase it, and you'll start believing in it."*
> —Jesse Owens

22

Hope on the Other Side

My son, pay attention to what I say;
turn your ear to my words.
Do not let them out of your sight,
keep them within your heart;
for they are life to those who find them
and health to one's whole body.
Above all else, guard your heart,
for everything you do flows from it.
Proverbs 4:20-23

Our heavenly Father knows our journeys. He knows all about the roads we have traveled, and he knows the paths that lie ahead.

The depths of God's understanding are unfathomable to me. More important, so are the depths of his love for all of us. In the middle of our humanness, our weaknesses and faults, he reaches out to give us strength.

Recently, I was talking with two other single moms. As they shared their stories, I gained an even deeper appreciation for God's unfathomable love. His sweet Spirit truly does help all things work together for good. These moms' kids are little miracles. They are gifts from above, and what the Lord is doing through these two families is a testimony to many.

One of the moms, Whitney, is recovering from drug addiction, a failed relationship, and a swarm of insecurities. Despite her trials, she told me that when she looks at her daughter, she sees a miracle. Listen to the hope in her words:

> Regardless of the unfortunate circumstances surrounding her conception, my child is a gift from God. God sees our family, and I know he has a special plan for my life, for all our lives. Many of us single moms deal with generational sins and destructive patterns in our families, but God can establish a new pattern.
>
> I know that a new beginning can start with me. Through Christ, we are all new creations. The chains of sin can no longer hold us. We are free to be the godly women God designed us to be. If we confess our sins to God, he will empower us to create a new life, a fresh path for our families.

Next, my friend Leilani shared some of her story. At one point, she entered a recovery program and faced a long separation from her son, who was only three years old at the time. Up to that point, she had never spent even a single day away from her boy, much less the twelve months required by the residential program she committed herself to. Here's what she said:

> When I entered the program, I didn't trust myself, much less other people. And I definitely did not trust God. I wondered how I was going to spend even one night apart from my boy. My heart ached for him more and more each

minute. I was so deeply heartbroken. Of course, this was exactly the kind of pain I needed if I was going to change my life. The pain helped me turn to God because he was the only one who could get me through the challenging year ahead of me.

During that year, I learned to get on my knees. I didn't realize it at first, but God was teaching me new coping skills. I was accustomed to using drugs, alcohol, and sex to cope, but my heavenly Father showed me a better way. Every day when I prayed, God pulled me up from my dire circumstances and into an amazing place of heavenly peace and rest. As the days rolled by, I found that I was actually craving my prayer times. Seeking God morning and night became my lifeline. It took time, but I started to trust God— with my son, my circumstances, our future together, and so much more.

God began to change my heart, *heal* my heart. He gave me new eyes to see my life. Day by day, I started living according to his perspective instead of mine.

During that year, God gave Leilani two key verses to trust in. Isaiah 55:9-11 assures us,

As the heavens are higher than the earth,
    so are my ways higher than your ways
    and my thoughts than your thoughts.
As the rain and the snow
    come down from heaven,

and do not return to it
without watering the earth
and making it bud and flourish,
so that it yields seed for the sower and bread for the eater,
so is my word that goes out from my mouth:
It will not return to me empty,
but will accomplish what I desire
and achieve the purpose for which I sent it.

Leilani explains, "That Scripture taught me that I am not *supposed* to understand everything about my circumstances and my relationships. God has a much bigger plan for me, and I need to trust him, even though I don't fully know or understand what is going on."

The second verse was Romans 8:28: "We know that in all things God works for the good of those who love him, who have been called according to his purpose." Leilani says,

> That verse assured me that God is in the business of divine reversals. Anything that the enemy intended for evil, God can and will use for the good! The people or circumstances that cause us harm? God will turn things around and create something good. This verse helped me trust in God deeper than ever. I allowed him to heal my past and help me rise above my circumstances. I still get on my knees every day in prayer. I always will.

These stories from two courageous single moms continue to inspire me every day. I hope they will do the same for you.

Heavenly Father,

I thank you for Whitney, Leilani, and the other single moms you have placed in my life. Thank you for their transparency and for their courage as they share their stories to help others.

Thank you, Lord, for your redeeming love in our lives. Thank you for blessing us with the miracles and the gifts you've given us through our children. Lord, I pray that the destructive patterns in our lives will be broken and will not be passed down to our sons and daughters. May a new pattern begin—a pattern of a new life in you.

Give us strength to get on our knees every day to be with you every morning and every evening.

In your precious name,

Amen.

23

Trust

Trust in the LORD with all your heart
and lean not on your own understanding;
in all your ways submit to him,
and he will make your paths straight.
Proverbs 3:5-6

*A*fter I went through my divorce, I heard this question a lot: "What are you going to do now?"

The only answer I could come up with was "I don't know." The same words came up a lot in my prayers. I would cry out to God, saying, "I don't know what to do, Lord!"

I felt him answer me. I felt him tell me that *he* knew what I should do. He reminded me that he knew the divorce was going to happen. It didn't take him by surprise. I sensed God asking me, "Becky, do you trust me?"

"But Lord," I would respond, "I am too broken and confused. I have too many questions. Why did this happen to our family? What happened to my 'happily ever after'? Am I being punished for something I did? And what about my boys? How can I be there for them? How can I be a good mom to them when I can barely breathe?"

I sensed that same response: "Do you trust me?"

I confess, it has not been easy for me to trust. I think it's hard for a lot of us single moms because the trust we once treasured has been broken. I don't know your story, but like me, you have probably felt betrayed in some way. How can anyone go through a divorce without suffering damage to her sense of trust?

Even now, two years after my divorce, I struggle sometimes when I try to find assurance that the Lord truly knows me. *Does he really understand me*, I wonder. *Is he repulsed by me? Is he going to abandon me because of my weaknesses and failings?*

That is why I try to wake up every morning and say, "I trust you, Lord." I highly recommend this. Say the words out loud.

"I trust you, Lord," I pray. "I trust you with my life, with my kids' lives, and with our future."

I encourage you to display these words where you will see them as you start your day: "I trust you, Lord." I know people who have this affirmation on their bathroom mirrors, on sticky notes in their cars, or as their screen savers. If you want to, tear off a corner of this page and write those words on it. Use it as your bookmark...or come up with another idea.

Pray the words whenever doubt attacks. Pray them when you are lonely or depressed. Just pray.

> *My heavenly Father,*
> *I am broken; I am weak. I have so many questions.*
> *But I do know you love me. This is not a surprise to*
> *you, that I would be in this place in life. You under-*
> *stand me, and you know what I am going through.*
> *Change my heart, Lord, to trust you. Repair the*

*wounded areas where trust has been broken. You
are Jehovah Rapha—the Healer. I trust you, Lord.
In your precious name,
Amen.*

24

A Heart's-Eye View

The LORD does not look at the things people look at.
People look at the outward appearance, but the LORD
looks at the heart.

1 Samuel 16:7

*F*or much of my life, I have struggled with low confidence and a lack of self-worth. So I guess it makes sense that my two sons struggle with these challenges as well.

I don't want my boys to feel the way I did when I was their age, so I try to use my experiences and what God is teaching me as I guide Caedmen and Eli.

My struggles started early. The middle child of three, I never really enjoyed being the center of attention. I grew especially uncomfortable when my peers teased me or joked around with me. I am sure their intentions were innocent enough, but being the butt of a joke caused me significant emotional stress.

When people started to joke or tease, blood rushed to my face and my heart began racing so hard I feared I would pass out. Even today I can feel the tension. It felt as if everyone was looking at me.

This response to teasing stretched from my early childhood through my college years.

My history has made it hard for me to share my single-mom

story, even to a few ladies from my church. In fact, sharing in a small-group setting is more terrifying to me than speaking at a large conference. It's as if my sense of inadequacy increases as the crowd size decreases! An intimate setting, with its close quarters and limited distractions, is more intimidating. I start to doubt that I have anything of value to share. I find myself wondering, *Does anybody really need to hear my story? Are my words going to make any difference?*

However, I've found that when it is time for me to share, the Holy Spirit can speak through me even as I struggle to find the right words. I have seen one of my crazy little stories break down walls so God can touch someone's heart.

Lots of self-help books are available for those of us who deal with esteem issues. Some of them say we need to love ourselves more, and that will help us regain a sense of self-worth. I don't want to speak for anyone else, but I have found my place, my voice, when I focus not on self-worth but on *God-worth*. God created me as a unique person with unique talents. He did the same for you. Really, that is all that matters. This is what I am trying to teach Caedmen and Eli as they grow from boys into young men.

I played soccer in high school and college. I remember wanting to do so well. I often sought affirmation from my dad. I recall him telling me, "Becky, you don't need to be the best soccer player on the field. Your self-worth shouldn't come from your sport. What matters is seeing yourself through God's eyes. Remember what he thinks of you. That is what truly matters."

Not my opinion of my worth, but his. Today, I share that wisdom with the two boys God has blessed me with.

We can all be targets of teasing, ridicule, or downright cruelty, especially in this age of ubiquitous social media. So let's all make the choice, every day, to make sure no one's insensitive words or actions take away our sense of God-worth.

"One great, strong, unselfish soul in every
community could actually redeem the world."
—Elbert Hubbard

25

On Teamwork and Home Turf

Two people are better off than one, for they can help each
other succeed. If one person falls, the other can reach out
and help. But someone who falls alone is in real trouble.
Ecclesiastes 4:9-10 NLT

This is my domain, my turf!" For many women, including single
moms, "my turf" means the kitchen or the pantry. And we don't
like that turf to be invaded.

Indeed, when someone messes with our food or beverages,
even the calmest among us can freak out. And many of us single moms are the most territorial of all moms, so our freak-outs
can be epic.

So perhaps we can best appreciate the horror endured by the
owners of a meat-packing plant when they discovered that someone—or *something*—was eating huge hunks of meat that were
hanging from hooks to age. Every morning, workers would enter
the plant and find that chunks of meat had been knocked to the
floor and devoured.

Desperate, they hired an exterminator to hide in the plant
overnight to catch the meat thief.

That exterminator was amazed by what he saw when night
fell. A swarm of rats snuck into the building. Then, one by one,
they formed a tall rat pyramid. Next, one rat scrambled its way

up the pyramid and leaped onto a hunk of beef. He then chewed the meat around the hook until the whole thing crashed to the floor. At that point, hundreds of rats pounced on their dinner and ate themselves silly.

As unappetizing as it might be, let's think about those clever rats for a bit. The rats at the bottom of the pyramid had to be strong and hold very still. The rats near the top had to be nimble as they climbed up, over, and around their rodent teammates. And even though they were oh-so-close to the meat, they had to keep their place so that one of their rat-buddies could accomplish the final task of crashing dinner to the floor.

The lesson here for today's single mom: Asking for help isn't a sign of weakness. Neither is being part of a team or a group. Sometimes working together is the smartest thing to do, even for the most independent-minded woman. Sometimes we need to share our turf if we want the best possible results.

The Bible tells us that two people working together can accomplish more than one person trying to go it alone. So don't be afraid to ask for help. And keep in mind that the person you seek help from today just might be the person who needs your help tomorrow!

> *Dear God,*
> *I thank you for my strong, independent spirit. It brings me dignity and confidence and purpose. At the same time, help me to remember that life is a team sport. Keep me from pride. Keep me from*

the kind of independence that leads to stubbornness. Make me willing to share my home turf when I need to. I love how the Bible is full of relationships. We are all, at various times, children, parents, brothers, and sisters. We are teachers and students. Help me to remember that two are better than one. And three or four? That can be better still.

I love you, my Father.

Amen.

26

Who Needs Enemies?

I tell you, love your enemies. Help and give without
expecting a return. You'll never—I promise—regret it.
Luke 6:35 MSG

Of all the Bible's commandments, perhaps none is tougher than "Love your enemies." We are told to go beyond tolerating them or doing them a few favors just to show what stellar people we are. No. Jesus said to love them. Those hateful, cruel, dishonest people. The church member who spreads hurtful rumors about you. The so-called friend who backstabs you. The boss who just won't give you a break. A former in-law who keeps blaming you for the end of a marriage. As I have mentioned earlier in this book, I have always struggled with criticism and teasing, but I think going through a divorce and becoming a single parent has made me more sensitive than ever.

Yes, loving an enemy is a hard, often unpleasant task for me. Perhaps the same is true for you. That's why prayer is the first step in the process. Pray that you'll have the grace, the will, and the patience to show love, and pray that your enemy will accept your efforts.

You might also need to pray about your own bitterness. (I certainly do.) That way, even if your prayers don't change an enemy's ugly qualities, they will still change you.

As you pray for your enemies and make efforts to bring peace to your relationships with them, you might come to realize that these people are no less attractive to God or loved by him than you are. Further, as you experience what hard work it is to love unlovable people, you might appreciate anew God's love for you.

> *Dear God,*
> *Help me respond lovingly to the difficult people in my life. May I remember that if I reach out in love to an adversary, I can reduce my list of enemies by one and gain a friend at the same time.*
> *Thank you for forgiving me.*
>
> *Amen.*

27

The Difference Between Whys and Wise

> As the heavens are higher than the earth,
> so are my ways higher than your ways
> and my thoughts than your thoughts.
>
> Isaiah 55:9

One of the joys of seeing my boys growing older is watching them become increasingly more proficient at grasping complex subjects. They are understanding more and more about spirituality, art, and life in general.

However, this wasn't always the case. I remember trying to explain how God was three beings in one and struggling to find an analogy that was both accurate and understandable.

They also struggled with the reasoning behind certain rules. Why is it that kids need to be wary of most strangers, but the ones in the church nursery are okay? Time and again, I realized my sons were not grasping what I was telling them, as evidenced by the number of times they uttered, "But *why*?" It can be so frustrating.

In our information-rich world, we have figured out so much. We have unraveled so many of life's tangled mysteries. But there is much more we don't understand. And just like a child who can't understand why she can't touch the moon, or why he can't eat candy for every meal, we question God about things that don't make sense to us. We demand to know why when life doesn't go according to our plan. At times like these, we forget that everything we know (or think we know) is a tiny droplet in the vast ocean of God's knowledge.

The Bible reminds us that God's ways are much higher than our ways and that we can comprehend only tiny shreds of his comprehensive master plan. Our responsibility is to follow him, and he will ultimately use everything for our good. This doesn't mean everything that happens in life *is* good. But it does mean that even the most frightening, terrible stories can work to our benefit when we place our trust in God and strive to obey him.

So, learn to appreciate life's questions. You can discover much about yourself and about life itself from the questions that emerge day to day. And remember that God, the Master Architect of the universe, has chosen to reach past the sun, the moon, and the stars to take your hand. The road ahead of you might be completely unfamiliar and intimidating. As a single mom, you might not know where the road will ultimately lead. But if you travel it hand in hand with God, your journey and your destination will be truly rewarding.

> *Father God,*
> *I am walking, even stumbling, along a rocky life path*
> *right now. But the terrain beneath my feet and the*
> *unknown paths ahead of me are no problem for you,*

the loving, powerful, and all-wise God who walks beside me and supports me and keeps me from falling. I am so grateful to you.

Amen.

28

Our Sympathetic Savior

We do not have a high priest who is unable to sympathize with our weaknesses, but one who in every respect has been tempted as we are, yet without sin. Let us then with confidence draw near to the throne of grace, that we may receive mercy and find grace to help in time of need.

Hebrews 4:15-16 ESV

*T*he Bible tells us that we are *guaranteed* difficulties in this world. As hard as this truth is, we wouldn't be so desperate for Christ if life was easy all the time.

My friend Deniece and I were talking about this truth when she said something that really challenged me. It might challenge you too, or even upset you, but please stay with me. Throughout my life, people have told me, "God never gives us more than we can handle." I heard it from the pulpit for years and years. And I heard it a lot during and right after my divorce. Here's the thing: It's not true. It's not in the Bible. You won't find it anywhere.

Yes, the Bible tells us we won't be tempted beyond what we can bear. First Corinthians 10:13 says, "No temptation has overtaken you except what is common to mankind. And God is faithful; he will not let you be tempted beyond what you can bear. But when you are tempted, he will also provide a way out so that you can endure it." However, temptations are not the same as hardships or tragedies.

The truth is that certain life events overwhelm our human capacity to handle them. I believe, however, that such tragedies reveal our weaknesses so God can demonstrate his strength in our lives. This means we never face a tragedy alone and we never suffer in vain. Our amazing God creates light in the darkest places. Our struggles can minister to others. They can serve as witnesses. And they can make us more compassionate and tender people. God brings beauty from ashes.

My heart is comforted by the assurance that Jesus knows the pain this world can bring. He knows it firsthand. He was rejected, abandoned, and tortured. He was despised and falsely accused. Yet in all these struggles, he modeled for us the security that comes from being "rooted and grounded in love" (Ephesians 3:17 ESV).

Jesus made it a regular practice to retreat and spend time alone with his heavenly Father. He craved the time to be still and seek the Father's will. He found nourishment and strength in these times of quiet spiritual intimacy. He found rest for his weary soul. He received the power to serve humankind and endure the suffering to come.

When we follow Christ's example and set aside quiet time with our heavenly Father, we are changed. We gain peace and strength. God wants us to come to him because he knows we are the ones who benefit. God appreciates and even craves our love, praise, and attention, but he is the one who sustains us, not the other way around.

Our God knows that when we experience his love, we experience security. He knows that when we approach him with thanksgiving and praise, our hearts and minds are renewed. He knows time in his presence sustains us. Only God fills every desire of our souls. He is not only capable but more than willing "to do far more abundantly beyond all that we ask or think" (Ephesians 3:20 ESV). His deep love for us puts down roots that penetrate and grasp our hearts. Nothing can separate us from this love. Nothing.

So, let us draw near to our heavenly Father. Let us ask, seek, and knock so we can receive, find, and have doors opened in our lives—doors only he can open.

When you experience tragedy that overwhelms you, remember that God will do something new in your life. He will sustain you. He will demonstrate his love and power. He will fill your cup so full that you will have an abundance of comfort and wisdom to share with others in their times of need.

> *Lord Jesus,*
> *Thank you for humbling yourself to walk this world*
> *as a man. Father, thank you for being compassion-*
> *ate toward your children. I ask you to strengthen*
> *me as I spend time in your presence. Make me more*
> *like your Son, Jesus. Assure me of your great love*
> *for me. I yearn to be rooted and grounded in that*
> *love. Renew my mind, fill my cup, and please use*
> *me, Lord. I long to bring glory to your name in all*

my circumstances. Show me your will. Guide my feet on the path you have for me. Use my hands for the work you have set before me.

Amen.

Scriptures for Meditation

During hard times in my life, the following Scriptures have been wonderful sources of comfort and meditation. Some are promises that can sustain us. Others are reminders that Jesus suffered too. I list them here in hopes that they might be valuable resources to you as well.

Isaiah 53:3	Mark 15:34	Romans 8:38-39
Matthew 7:7	John 16:33	2 Corinthians 1:3-4
Matthew 26:31	Romans 5:3-4	Ephesians 3:16-21
Mark 6:4	Romans 8:28	James 1:2-5

29

Our God Rewards Faithful Effort

I will wait on the LORD...
And I will hope in Him.
Here am I...
Isaiah 8:17-18 NKJV

*H*ave you ever heard one of your girlfriends, relatives, or even a date say something like this? "I could have done something really great in life; I just never got that big break."

The sad thing is that so many people *could* have accomplished something great if they had seized all their little opportunities and breaks instead of waiting for the Big One.

God blesses us when we live gratefully and purposefully, whatever our circumstances. He blesses us when we grab opportunities—even those that don't come in our preferred size and shape.

Consider this example. A young woman dreamed of writing for the masses, but that dream seemed a world away from her actual job as a lowly copy editor for a small-town newspaper. She felt fortunate to have *any* job in publishing. After all, one of her college instructors had once told her, "Forget about being a writer."

Nonetheless, she graduated with an English degree and found a paper that would pay her (modestly) for her writing skills. But those skills were confined to editing the obituaries—one of the lowest rungs on the newspaper ladder.

Meanwhile, the woman married, and she and her husband tried to conceive—without success. Their family doctor told them they would never be able to have a baby. So they adopted a daughter. Less than a year later, the woman got pregnant. In fact, she got pregnant four times during the next four years. Sadly, only two of those babies survived childbirth.

For the next 20 years, this writer, wife, and mother toiled at low-level newspaper jobs. Finally, she convinced one of her editors to let her write a weekly humor column—for three dollars per piece. A year later, the editor sweetened the pot. Somewhat. He bumped the column's frequency to three times a week. And he told her he would try to syndicate the column to other papers.

More than 900 newspapers said yes.

For the next 30 years, Erma Bombeck wrote her column, which was eagerly read by more than 30 million people in the United States and Canada. Bestselling books followed. Her face graced the cover of *Time* and other national publications. She was awarded a host of honorary degrees. She was perhaps America's best-known humor writer. She was a favorite of my mom, and I grew to enjoy Erma's brand of warm humor just as much.

Erma Bombeck wrote with wit and charm despite trials in her personal life. She endured breast cancer and kidney failure. On the professional front, she wrote a sitcom that was canned after just a few episodes. She penned a Broadway play that never opened.

During the last few years of her life, she faced daily dialysis.

But she kept on writing. She made America laugh and sometimes cry. Her passing at age 69 was national news. America knew it had lost one of its most entertaining and gracious voices.

Bombeck showed us how to keep our shortcomings in perspective: "What you have to tell yourself is, 'I am not a failure. I failed at something.' There's a big difference."

Erma Bombeck's life is a lesson to us all, including us single moms. Our failings do not make us failures. Divorce does not make us failures. Sometimes, a failure is just the beginning of a great life story. Don't let setbacks derail your dreams.

Heavenly Father,
Erma Bombeck once said, "It takes a lot of courage to show your dreams to someone else." Please give me the courage to hold on to my dreams and share them. Give me courage in the face of setbacks and disappointment. My hope is in you, and that holy hope can never be crushed.

Amen.

30

On Grief and Belief

God blesses those who mourn,
for they will be comforted.
Matthew 5:4 NLT

We live in a fallen world, and as a result, we all experience pain. Many of the single moms I know understand the hurt of a relationship destroyed. Others have experienced the death of a husband, often due to unforeseen and tragic circumstances. The loss of a loved one will, most likely, affect every one of us at some point in life. Fortunately, God is Lord over all of it—the pain, the questions, the helpless feelings.

God never said our journey would be without stumbles, without heartaches, without deep loss. From our earthly perspective, the loss is sometimes all we can see. Yet from God's eternal, all-knowing perspective, the view is different.

This is not to say the Lord doesn't hurt with us and for us. Remember the famously shortest verse in the Bible? John 11:35 says, "Jesus wept." Why did Jesus cry?

In the story, Jesus's good friend Lazarus had died. Of course, Jesus grieved the loss of a friend. We can appreciate that. However, Jesus knew that in a few seconds, he would tell Lazarus to get up and walk out of the tomb. He knew this tragic story would end in victory.

Is it possible that Jesus was so sad because his loved ones were grieving and in pain? He knew Lazarus would be alive and well in moments, yet Jesus agonized for his friends. He felt their pain. He wasn't crying for himself and his own sadness; he was crying for his people. He was crying for people just like us!

Our Lord knows when we are hurting, and he is there for us every second, through every tear.

Our duty as followers is to seek God's will and purpose in everything. We may see only a tiny piece of his plan, but he sees every effect, every ripple throughout eternity. Someday we will see how God orchestrated it all through history and through the moments of our lives. Even the tough moments.

For now, we can rest in knowing God's plan is good and his promises are true. He will make good on his promise to work all things for our good if we love and serve him. He will be our Comforter and Deliverer in our times of utmost pain and grief.

God understands that this world can hurt sometimes. But this is not our ultimate home. Heaven is a real place, a place of complete joy, and we will see it soon enough. Then we will grieve no more. And our Lord Jesus will grieve no more for us.

Our loving Lord,
Let us rest today in the knowledge that we cannot
go anywhere, even the depths of despair, where your
love and compassion cannot reach.

                                     Amen.

31

The Power of Praise

The Spirit of the Sovereign LORD is on me,
because the LORD has anointed me
to proclaim good news to the poor.
He has sent me to bind up the brokenhearted,
to proclaim freedom for the captives
and release from darkness for the prisoners,
to proclaim the year of the LORD's favor
and the day of vengeance of our God,
to comfort all who mourn,
and provide for those who grieve in Zion—
to bestow on them a crown of beauty
instead of ashes,
the oil of joy
instead of mourning,
and a garment of praise
instead of a spirit of despair.
They will be called oaks of righteousness,
a planting of the LORD
for the display of his splendor.

Isaiah 61:1-3

This Scripture inspired "The Garment of Praise," a classic old worship song that I know will stick with me forever. It's been decades since I first heard the lyrics, but I can still sing them. I love the concept of putting on a garment of praise instead of a spirit of despair.

Ever since I was a little girl, my mom taught me, "If you are down, discouraged, or just feeling melancholy, start to worship. Lift up your voice in praise to God." For years now, I have taken these words to heart and engaged in the practice of praise that I learned from my wonderful mother. Whenever I follow her advice, I can lift my heart above my troubles.

I wish I put the concept into practice all the time instead of just *most* of the time. On certain days, I roll out of bed feeling heavy and overwhelmed. Some mornings start off rough. My boys are fighting because one of them committed the heinous crime of looking at the other the wrong way. And I feel defeated before the day has even begun.

I know I am not the only mom who deals with days like these. Every one of us has those mornings when the challenges ahead tempt us to pull the covers over our heads and wait until we feel better about life in general. On mornings like that, I know I need praise in my life. I play some praise and worship music, and as I sing along, my mood changes. Always. I am drawn into the Lord's presence, and that is always a good place to be.

The practice of praise is so powerful. I love the story of Paul and Silas (see Acts 16:22-26), who sang hymns and praises to God even though they were imprisoned in a dark, oppressive dungeon. The duo's songs lifted their own spirits as well as those of their fellow prisoners.

Eventually, an earthquake shook open the dungeon doors,

and the prisoners' chains were loosened. Everyone was set free, not just Paul and Silas.

What an amazing and powerful truth this story provides for us: Praising God loosens chains. It opens doors, sometimes *literally*.

As a single mom, my chains are the wounds of my past and my own negative thoughts. But God can set me free. When I am trapped by my perceived inadequacies, he is there. When I get frustrated because my sons aren't getting along, I put on that garment of praise, and I find myself dwelling with the Lord instead of dwelling on my resentment. Whatever the situation, praise can help you overcome!

Psalm 22:3 assures us that God is enthroned on the praise of his people. Let's make it a habit to invite him into our darkest moments through praise.

> *Heavenly Father,*
> *I want to praise you not just with my words but with my life. Time and again, I have seen that there is power in praising you. Mighty changes happen. Chains are loosened. The weight of sadness melts away. Energy and zeal take its place.*
>
> *May I offer you a sacrifice of praise today. Please draw near to me and dwell with me. And may my boys see and know the power of praise and worship in their lives.*
>
> *Thank you, precious Lord!*
>
> *Amen.*

32

From One Single Mom to Another

So above all, constantly chase after the realm of God's
kingdom and the righteousness that proceeds from him.
Then all these less important things will be given to you
abundantly. Refuse to worry about tomorrow, but deal
with each challenge that comes your way, one day at a
time. Tomorrow will take care of itself.

Matthew 6:33-34 TPT

One of the reasons I have such a close bond with my mother is that she was a single mom too. She and my biological father divorced when my two sisters and I were very young—five and a half, two and a half, and six months. My mother was remarried (about two years later) to a wonderful man who happens to be a pastor at Gateway of Praise Worship Center in Divide, Colorado. He and my mom have been great marriage role models for my sisters and me.

As you can imagine, the divorce was devastating to my mom. She wasn't sure how we would survive financially. She wasn't sure what our future would look like. But day by day, she put her trust in the Lord. My mom is a woman of prayer. Whenever we were driving and passed an accident, she started praying for the victims and the first responders.

If I were to call her today with some challenge, she would say,

"Let's pray." I have lost count of the times she has prayed over me and my boys through the years. She has instilled in me and my sisters the need to pray and the effectiveness of our prayers. I am trying to instill this in my own boys as well. I am so thankful for every opportunity to pray with them and for them.

After my parents' divorce, my mom and we three young girls moved into my maternal grandparents' home in Washington State. We had a roof over our heads, but my mom still felt hopeless. "I knew I was going to have to find a job so I could support my girls," she recalls, "but I was a stay-at-home mom. I didn't have job skills. During this time, Isaiah 54:4-5 became my lifeline."

> Do not be afraid; you will not be put to shame.
>   Do not fear disgrace; you will not be humiliated.
> You will forget the shame of your youth
>   and remember no more the reproach of your widowhood.
> For your Maker is your husband—
>   the LORD Almighty is his name—
> the Holy One of Israel is your Redeemer;
>   he is called the God of all the earth.

"That Scripture reminded me that our Almighty God said he would be my defender. He would be a Father to my little girls. We learned to rest in this promise, especially when we found ourselves needing clothes, food, or other necessities. We would pray together as a family, and we saw simple miracles happen as a result."

My mom told me about a time when my sisters and I all needed new pajamas but she had no way to afford them. We all prayed together. Soon, we found a set of three new pajamas at our front door. No card, no note. "It was as if God had sent them from heaven," according to Mom. (We discovered later that the PJs were a gift from someone in our church.)

Other times, we would open the door to find a box of groceries waiting for us. Our family felt loved and protected and cared for by God and his people. "During that time," my mother explains, "I truly learned to pray about everything and not to worry."

In Philippians 4:6, Paul encourages us to "be saturated in prayer throughout each day." My mom lived this principle, and she has passed it down to her three daughters. Every day we strive to offer our "faith-filled requests before God with overflowing gratitude" (TPT).

When we do this, God's peace, which transcends all human understanding, guards our hearts and minds in Christ Jesus. I pray God's peace upon you, today and always.

> *Dear caring Father,*
> *Thank you for watching over me ever since I was a little girl. Thank you for my mom. I am amazed at the ways you have provided for me and those I love. Please continue watching over us, and help us to be generous with what we have. And whether we find ourselves rich or poor on any given day, let us be thankful and hopeful, no matter what.*
>
> *Amen.*

33

Renew Me

If anyone is in Christ, the new creation has come: The
old has gone, the new is here! All this is from God, who
reconciled us to himself through Christ.
2 Corinthians 5:17-18

*I*t just so happens that I am writing about renewal on January 1.
I wish I could say I planned this, but no.

I am thinking about New Year's resolutions and wondering
if they are still "a thing." But regardless of whether we make formal resolutions, we all have ideas about what we want to change
in our lives. Most of us have goals, even if they are fuzzy and
unformed and vague. Many of these center on our health—
losing weight, exercising more, scheduling a visit to the doctor,
and eating a healthful diet. You know the drill.

It's easy to get cynical about health-related resolutions and
their (usually) short lifespan, but nothing is wrong with wanting
to improve our physical health. Our bodies are God's temples, after
all, and I believe he wants us to treat them well. The healthier we
are, the better our chances of fulfilling God's purposes for our lives.

That said, I believe there are higher priorities for us to pursue.
I went walking this morning, and I started to wonder why more
people don't resolve to pray more, to strive to hear God more
clearly. To be more intentional about their spiritual lives.

I asked myself, "What does God want to renew in me day by day?" I decided to pick out three simple things I could do today to be more in step with his will and his Spirit.

First, I decided to compliment the cashier at my local grocery store. I resolved to say something that would evoke a smile. Next, I decided to make an extra-special breakfast for my kids. And finally, I made room in the day to call a friend I hadn't talked to in a while. I simply wanted to tell her that she was on my heart and ask how I could pray for her.

I know that if I could do a few simple things like this every day, I could take my eyes off myself and my circumstances. I would be more open to what God is saying to me. Whenever I do this, I find myself more and more blessed, even though finding blessing for myself wasn't the goal!

Don't wait for New Year's Day to start seeing yourself and others through God's eyes. You will be amazed at the results.

Dear Lord,

I know you are delighted when I pray for positive changes in my life. I know you want to see me grow. Please refresh me today. Renew my passion to serve and bless others. Open my eyes and my ears and my heart. I want to love others the way you love me. I ask you to put people in my path who need you; please give me what I need to help them.

I ask these things in your precious name.

Amen.

34

On Influencing Friends and Family

Get rid of all bitterness, rage and anger, brawling and slander, along with every form of malice. Be kind and compassionate to one another, forgiving each other, just as in Christ God forgave you.

Ephesians 4:31-32

*H*ave you ever heard a joke that you just didn't get? If you asked the joke-teller for an explanation, chances are that the explanation did not suddenly make the joke funny. Getting a "nuts and bolts" lecture about something—whether it's a joke or the inner workings of a car engine—isn't the same thing as being moved, entertained, or inspired.

As Christian moms, we often want to influence our friends, family, and coworkers who don't share our faith. We collect evidence, counterarguments, Bible verses, and all kinds of other tools to unleash the next time the opportunity arises. We are full of explanations. We have our proof texts in place. We are wired for witnessing.

Unfortunately, you can win a debate about God and lose a chance to draw someone to him. Many a Christian has laid out an airtight case for her faith, only to hear, "I don't care about all that. I don't believe in God, no matter what you say about him. I just don't want to be a Christian."

Faith is often more about the will than the intellect. Jesus didn't say, "I will out-debate everyone so they will have no choice but to believe in me." Rather, he said, "I will *draw* all people to myself." And he drew people through his love, his compassion, and his sacrifice.

Conversely, a war of words is highly *unlikely* to draw someone to faith. Or to spark a major change in one's life. But we can each do our part to bring others to our Savior. Love one another. Forgive one another. Show grace. Work to gain heavenly approval, not mere human approval. Be humble. Be a peacemaker. Just imagine what those outside the church would think of Christians if these traits were our hallmarks.

People can argue about apologetics and proof texts and "clobber passages," but who can argue with a life lived Jesus's way and the impact it has? That kind of living has a way of drawing people in the right direction. About this, there is no argument.

Heavenly Father,

As I interact with people in my life, may I be a source of light, not a source of conflict and bitterness. I love to spend time with people who are kind, gracious, patient, and wise, no matter what their religious beliefs are. Let me be that kind of person. May I reflect Jesus in all I do and say.

In your name,
Amen.

35

The Making of an Encourager

Therefore encourage one another and build each other
up, just as in fact you are doing.
1 Thessalonians 5:11

*H*ere's how to identify someone who needs encouragement," goes the old saying. "That person is breathing."

Especially in today's age of cynicism and instant internet criticism, encouragement matters more than ever. I know how much it has meant to me, especially in the months since my divorce.

Encouragement helps take away the sting of that cruel comment one might hear at work, at home, or on social media. Sometimes encouragement renews hopes and dreams. It can even change a life. Encouragement is a critical need of every person, family, school, community, and workplace. It's so needed in churches as well. It saddens me that so many churches are sources of judgment, criticism, and political partisanship, but encouragement is rare.

Everyone needs encouragement, and everyone who receives encouragement is changed by it. To encourage people is, by definition, to help them gain *courage*, courage they might not otherwise find.

Don't we all need encouragement to face the day, to do what's right, to make a difference? Many of us moms are naturally good encouragers, but this is a gift anyone can share. At its heart, encouragement is all about communicating a person's value. When people feel valuable, they feel capable—and most of all, loved.

As Zig Ziglar put it, "You never know when a moment and a few sincere words can have an impact on a life."

As you seek to encourage your children, your coworkers, your friends, or whomever, look for opportunities like these:

> When people are struggling to do the right thing, stand with them.
>
> When people are striving to face a big challenge, empower them.
>
> When people are working toward a goal, motivate them.
>
> When people are looking for a place to belong, welcome them.
>
> When people are seeking some recognition or validation, honor them.
>
> When people are hurting, comfort them.

Indeed, encouragement can take many forms. If you are stuck for ideas, think about what inspires and encourages you. And what inspires those precious kids in your life? A handwritten note or card? A surprise phone call? A clever text or email message? An invitation to lunch or coffee? A personalized gift basket? Gestures like these can do so much to bless others—and you as well. It just takes a bit of time and effort.

Today, why not give someone (and yourself) the gift of encouragement?

> *"We can all remember a time when someone encouraged us and made a difference in our lives. It may be just a moment, but this encouragement could last a lifetime."*
>
> —Megan Shull

36

May We Live to Forgive

If you forgive other people when they sin against you,
your heavenly Father will also forgive you.
But if you do not forgive others their sins,
your Father will not forgive your sins.
Matthew 6:14-15

I was just checking a few versions of the Bible, and most of them mention the words "forgive," "forgiveness," and "forgiven" about 200 times. Clearly, a forgiving spirit is something God wants us to strive for. But this isn't easy, especially when we feel so wounded, so unfairly treated by someone. Whenever I find it especially hard to forgive a friend, family member, or coworker, I remember the words of Colossians 3:13: "Bear with each other and forgive one another...Forgive as the Lord forgave you." That puts everything into perspective for me.

I know that those of us who are single moms because of divorce have varied stories, but I have seen a common theme: We struggle to forgive our exes, and we struggle to forgive ourselves. For some, that struggle can last for years. Perhaps as you read these words, this struggle is ongoing for you.

Recently I was talking with my friend Michele. As she shared her story, I was amazed and encouraged by her story of forgiveness. She endured hard times, but the Lord was faithful to her. His hands were supporting her even before she realized she needed his divine support.

She became a single mom in 1974. If you recall that era, you know that single moms were a rarity. Her husband walked out without warning just before Christmas. They had just purchased a home together. Their daughter, Ali, was only 14 months old.

Just wait—the story gets even more tragic. Michele and her husband lived in a small town and worked for the same school district. When Michele's husband, a teacher, left his family, he moved in with his teacher's aide.

Thus, Michele had to encounter her ex and his new love interest every workday. "I would go home for the weekend," she explained to me, "and start to feel semi-normal. Then Monday morning would come, and I would see the two of them at school. That would start a decline that lasted all week. Many times, I wondered how I would survive if not for my little daughter, who needed me to take care of her, to be responsible for her."

Michele didn't have a personal relationship with Jesus at the time, but she explains, "I did believe in God and that Jesus was his Son. I remember praying a lot and relying on friends for support."

Thanks to those friends, Michele says she didn't suffer the loneliness many single moms experience. Besides, she says, "My husband and I had been together for only two years, and he had not been the best spouse and father, to say the least. That lessened my struggle somewhat."

For the next nine years, Michele lived the single-mom life. Her ex never paid a penny of child support, and he chose to have almost no contact with Ali. "Before I married him," Michele recalls, "I knew he had three sons from a previous marriage. He had very little to do with them. You would think I would have gotten the hint!"

Because of her ex's lack of involvement, Michele raised Ali without her father's input—or interference. "That turned out to be a blessing in the long run," she confesses, "but I was sad for Ali because she didn't have a father figure in her life. Eventually, however, we both came to terms with that reality. In time, she came to agree with me that her biological father's presence wouldn't have made her life better."

Michele worked full-time as a speech pathologist. When she wasn't working and Ali wasn't in day care or in school, they were joined at the hip. "It was the post-hippie era," she says, "and my life was...let's just say, pretty loose. But I was never irresponsible when it came to my daughter's welfare. Every day I told her and showed her that she was loved. To this day, I know that commitment made our relationship strong, and I know it helped her grow up to be the wonderful woman she is today. Whatever faults I might have had, I was honest, loving, and involved in my relationship with Ali. And I was responsible at my job."

Michele confesses that the year after her husband left was a dark time. "My work and my friends kept me going," she says. "My friends listened to my story and my pain time and time again. Then, finally, one of those good friends said to me, 'Michele, it's been almost a year. It's time you got over it. It's time to stop talking about your ex and just move on.'

"You know what? He was right. I stopped talking about my ex. I stopped reliving the past. I got over it!

"Today, I am a believer in God. He has given me the strength to forgive Ali's father for the many things he did—and the many things he failed to do. I am at peace with the past. I love, cherish, and praise God for the present. I thank him for Ali, her husband, and their two daughters—my grandkids! We are also neighbors. We are a whole and healthy family!"

As a single mom from a more recent generation, I found Michele's story so inspiring. I hope you do too.

I asked Michele to create a prayer to end this devotion. Here it is.

> *Lord,*
> *You are the God who renews me and puts passion in*
> *my heart. You are delighted when I pray for change,*
> *and you want to bring change in me. Lord, refresh*
> *me today. Open my ears to hear your voice, open my*
> *eyes to see what you see, and open my heart to love*
> *like you love. Put people in my path who need you.*
> *In your precious name,*
> *Amen.*

37

Who's in Your Company?

Walk with the wise and become wise,
for a companion of fools suffers harm.
Proverbs 13:20

*F*ew of life's choices are tougher or more important than one's choice of friends. The choice isn't always easy. After all, Jesus spent time with people of low reputation—even to the point of being called a lowlife himself.

On the other hand, the Bible is full of advice like this: "Do not be misled: 'Bad company corrupts good character.' Come back to your senses as you ought, and stop sinning; for there are some who are ignorant of God" (1 Corinthians 15:33-34).

So how do we do both at the same time? How do we follow Jesus's example of inclusiveness while surrounding ourselves with the kind of people who positively influence us?

First, we should spend as much time as possible with godly people who will encourage us to grow closer to our Creator. We all need people who provide a good example and hold us accountable if our behavior starts to slide.

Second, as we befriend troubled people, we must be careful to do so on our terms as much as possible. I know some Christian single moms who frequent bars and clubs that have questionable reputations. These same moms tell their kids that an unsupervised party is not a good place to hang with troubled friends; neither is a car driven by someone who is intoxicated or underage. However, these moms have developed a blind spot when it comes to some of their own choices.

Finally, you must continue to monitor your friendships and be able to give a clear-eyed assessment of where they are leading you and vice versa. Are you influencing your friends for good? Are they asking more questions about God than they did days and weeks ago? Are they picking up good habits from you, or is the reverse happening?

In other words, are *you* the one being changed? Has your language, your attitude, or your behavior changed for the worse? Are you dabbling in websites that would have been off the menu a few months ago? If that's the case, it might be time to find yourself a new "company."

Heavenly Father,
As a single mom, I am always excited to make new friends. I need that adult interaction. But please guide me so I choose my friends with thought and care—and prayer. Keep me from any friendship that might bring heartache into my life and the life of my kids. I don't want to judge others, but I don't want to compromise my values either. May I look to you always for guidance.

In your wise name,
Amen.

38

The Hard Work of Love

"Though the mountains be shaken
and the hills be removed,
yet my unfailing love for you will not be shaken
nor my covenant of peace be removed,"
says the LORD, who has compassion on you.
Isaiah 54:10

What is love? Almost every pop song mentions the concept. It's a major theme of movies and TV shows as well. Unfortunately, much of what you see and hear in modern media isn't real love. The love many pop singers profess, for example, is often a selfish obsession, lacking depth. Or it's a whim, usually driven by physical attraction. "I love you, baby!" in a top-40 song is better translated, "I am hot for you at this present moment—until someone more attractive comes into the picture. Or I get bored with you."

God, the author of love, didn't design it to be a mere feeling. Love is a decision, an act of the will. Love is a marathon, not a sprint. It requires focus and constant effort. True love is caring about another person—a friend, parent, sibling, child, or significant other—even if your love isn't reciprocated or even appreciated. Love is a commitment that doesn't fade, regardless of consequences. It's a sacrifice. It's something you do even when you don't feel like it.

Real love is what Jesus displayed for the world when he chose to sacrifice himself for all of us. And he made this choice knowing that many would spurn or belittle his supreme sacrifice. Further, he knew that no one deserved this great gift of love. He knows the selfishness of the human heart. He knows every awful thing about every single person who has ever lived or ever will live. Yet he still gave himself up.

The Lord of all creation, who knew you even before you were born, has decided to love you. Despite your mistakes. Despite the indifference you might feel toward him sometimes. God loves you. He is committed to you. He will faithfully forgive, unconditionally accept, and perfectly love you always. He makes the effort every day.

So don't be swayed by the media depictions of fake love. You have the real thing, direct from the Source. This is the kind of love we should demonstrate to others. And this is the kind of love we should look for in our romantic relationships!

Loving Father,

I am thankful that Christ's love will carry me through whatever happens, even if today it feels impossible to make it to tomorrow. Heavenly love never fails. What a miraculous blessing!

I love you, Lord.

Amen.

39

Becoming Simply Successful

What does the LORD require of you?
To act justly and to love mercy
and to walk humbly with your God.

Micah 6:8

*T*oo often, the life of a twenty-first-century single mom is anything but simple. Our days, weeks, months, and years can become a tornado of busy schedules, interpersonal conflicts, and to-do lists that never get to-done. It seems that we can spend most of our lives somewhere in between problems and opportunities—not knowing which to attack first.

Just think about how much of life is "in between." In between things like meetings, conference calls, medical appointments, errand-running, kid-transporting, and home repairs—whether we are doing the repairing or waiting on the "experts."

There must be a simpler way to navigate this busy thing called life, especially for those of us who often do it alone.

Writer Linda Ellis, author of the popular poem "The Dash," says the key is living to make a difference. She contends, "It's not the date you were born or the date you died that really matters. It's the dash between those years and what you do with it—to make a difference with your life."

What about us, my single-mom colleagues? Are we truly

making a difference? Sometimes we need to hit the pause button to answer this question correctly, to ask ourselves, *What are the things in my life that feed and inspire me? And what should I be doing to feed, inspire, and serve others, especially my kids? What can I say to them? What can I do for them?*

The answers to these questions give us fresh perspective and renewed energy. Yes, some of the mundane tasks still need to be done, but perhaps there is a way to do them with kindness and creativity and patience. For example, maybe that dreaded weekly meeting is a chance to tell a coworker how much you appreciate her expertise or even her smile. Maybe driving your kid to soccer practice can be a chance for a heartfelt, meaningful conversation—instead of one more frantic chore, with both of you lost in your own thoughts, worries, and to-do lists.

When we rise above the clutter and noise, we find that it's the simple little things—the simple little actions and simple little words—that constitute so much of life. They keep us going. They help us keep *others* going.

True, life is busy sometimes. Life is complicated. But with the right perspective and sense of purpose, it can be simpler. And simply more rewarding.

> *"Every person has a longing to be significant;*
> *to make a contribution; to be a part of*
> *something noble and purposeful."*
>
> —John Maxwell

40

Lead to Succeed

Rebuke the wise, and they will love you.
Instruct the wise and they will be wiser still;
teach the righteous and they will add to their learning.
Proverbs 9:8-9

*A*s you might recall from earlier in this book, I love to hike. Give me a mountain trail or a path through a forest, and I'm happy. Especially if I have my canine hiking partner, Keva, by my side.

On one hike through a heavily wooded area, I noticed a crooked tree. It looked like a lowercase letter "r." I moved in a little closer and saw that someone had placed a large upright pole and tied it to the tree with ropes. Clearly, this was an attempt to straighten out the crooked tree as it grew.

However, as I stepped back for a broader view, I could tell that the upper part of the tree had already veered away from its base. Nothing was going to correct the misdirected growth. The crooked part of the tree was too far from the corrective pole.

This story carries a lesson for today's single mom. No matter your situation, you are probably a leader of some sort, just as I am. The single moms I know are coaches, managers, community organizers, city council members, and heads of committees at their churches or civic organizations...in addition to leading their families!

As a leader, you have a responsibility to guide those you lead. But it's hard to correct and redirect people—whether they are your kids, someone else's kids, your employees, or the folks on the church finance committee.

After all, who wants to hurt someone's feelings or risk harming a relationship? Unfortunately, those risks come with the territory. As a leader, you must keep people and projects on track. That means regular and consistent feedback even when that feedback is not all sunshine, confetti frosting, and rainbows.

Otherwise, people and projects can veer off course. And as that tree reminded me, the longer problems go unchecked, the harder it is to correct them.

If you struggle with giving what some business consultants call "negative feedback," consider this: You do people a favor when you set clear expectations for them. Without such expectations, how can someone know if he or she is succeeding?

This is true for the adults who call you "boss" as well as the kids who call you "mom." By the way, whenever I give correction, I remember the words of the great basketball coach John Wooden: "A leader is someone who can give correction without causing resentment."

When you must correct or discipline someone, make sure your words and actions show you *care.* You care enough to keep someone on the right path and moving at the right speed. (That's what made John Wooden such a successful coach.)

With prayer, care, and tact, a strong female leader can help others grow to become all they can be.

Dear Creator and Sustainer,

Sometimes leadership is simply hard. Whether at home or elsewhere, empower me to lead with integrity and wisdom. And especially when it comes to my kids, please prevent my emotions from getting the best of me. When I must speak hard truths, may I speak the truth in love, as your Word instructs. Let me speak love, peace, grace, and encouragement into the lives of others.

Let me lead by example, a loving and godly example.

In your name,
Amen.

41

Springtime in the Rockies

See, I am doing a new thing!
Now it springs up; do you not perceive it?
I am making a way in the wilderness
and streams in the wasteland.

Isaiah 43:19

*D*uring the winters in our little mountain town, we can wake up in the morning to find ourselves almost buried in snow. Once the calendar flips to December (or sometimes November), we can go months without seeing a hint of dry ground. I love living in ski country, but I always feel blessed when I experience the first signs of spring. To us mountain folk, the sound of snow melting and dripping from trees and rooftops is sweet music. We feel joy at a single crocus emerging from the snow after a long winter's slumber.

When that blanket of white finally melts, we pale, sun-starved people rush outdoors. Even if it's only 40 degrees or so, it feels like summer to us. That's why you can see Coloradans running around in T-shirts and shorts when there's still snow all around us. We are *that* hungry for sunshine.

For me, the red-winged blackbirds are a sure sign that spring is here. I love their beautiful songs. I love looking skyward and seeing flocks of my winged friends returning to the majestic trees.

Their calls feel like official announcements of the changing of the seasons.

In addition to my boys and my dog, three parakeets call our house their home. (Because it isn't challenging *enough* to keep the house clean.) Parakeets are messy little things who toss their seeds all over the place. But every morning when I uncover them, they start chirping, as if to welcome the day. And I smile at another new beginning. I hear my birds and start thinking about possibilities, about the chance to grow spiritually.

I say a prayer, thanking God for his blessings. I put my hope, and my family's hope, in him, and I am able to greet the new day with joy.

> *"There are far, far better things ahead than any we leave behind."*
>
> —C.S. Lewis

42

Perfect Love

But you, dear friends, by building yourselves up in your
most holy faith and praying in the Holy Spirit, keep yourselves in God's love as you wait for the mercy of our Lord
Jesus Christ to bring you to eternal life.

Jude 20-21

We used to own a wood pellet stove. We loved the heat it provided but not the task of cleaning the glass door, which was like
a magnet for thick, black soot that swallowed the light from the
fire. We could barely see the crackling orange-yellow flames for
all the dark residue.

No high-tech cleaning solution known to humanity could
get that glass clean. I had to scrape the gunk away with a razor
blade. One day as I was scraping away, I thought about how the
stove residue is like worry, anxiety, and panic. It swallows our
light; it blocks our joy. I know I have let darkness accumulate in
my life. Before long, the buildup is so significant that it's overwhelming and downright terrifying.

I should stop and confess that initially, I didn't want to
include this chapter in the book. I find it hard to talk frankly
about my anxiety. However, I know that many single moms face
this struggle, so I want to be transparent, just like that glass on
the wood stove after a thorough cleaning.

Since my divorce, I have battled attacks of overwhelming anxiety. I lie awake in bed, trying to get some sleep. It has been hard to get used to sleeping alone after so many years of sharing a bed with a husband. And even when I could drift off to sleep, I would awaken to a feeling of unspeakable darkness and a heavy weight on my chest. I struggle to explain just how terrifying this is to me. I know this is an attack from the enemy, but the attack is so oppressive that sometimes I can barely manage to pray.

When I got scared as a child, my mom would encourage me to recite 2 Timothy 1:7: "God has not given us a spirit of fear, but of power and of love and of a sound mind" (NKJV).

As a young girl, I focused on replacing my spirit of fear with the spirit of love. That's what helped me most. As an adult, I find myself focusing on replacing fear with a sound mind. When panic hits, I pray, "Lord, please protect my mind! Please protect the *sound mind* you have given me."

To compound my struggle, I also suffer from terrible migraine headaches. They first invaded my life during my teen years, but they got much worse as I became an adult. Over the past ten years, they have grown in intensity. If you are a migraine sufferer as well, you know how debilitating they can be. I just don't feel like myself when I have a migraine even though I might appear to be okay.

My migraines can last for as many as five days. My boys have grown accustomed to seeing their mom in horrible pain. That fact makes me so sad. I simply can't enjoy life with my sons while I am in the grip of a migraine. I try to endure the suffering as best I can, but my most recent episode sent me to the emergency room.

While I was in the ER receiving treatment, I experienced an anxiety attack, much like the ones that had been waking me up at night. I started shaking uncontrollably. It was awful. Then I thought of my mom and that Scripture she taught me. I took a deep breath and said, "God has not given me a spirit of fear, but of power and of love and of a sound mind."

I prayed, "Dear Lord, please give me a sound mind so that I will not fear."

I prayed these words because fear is one of my greatest weaknesses. Perhaps the same is true for you. Fear comes from the father of lies. He speaks death, telling us, *You are crazy, and you're never going to get through this ordeal. You are not a good role model for your children. You are weak. You are a hopeless case!*

But, thank God, perfect love casts out fear! (See 1 John 4:18.) All humans are flawed, so no one (family member, friend, or boyfriend!) can give us perfect love—but our heavenly Father can.

Of course, I am so grateful that I have friends and family who try to help me with these struggles. I know they want what's best for me; I know they want to help me. And it means so much to have someone listen to me when I am afraid or when I am filled with negative thoughts and I simply need to vent...even when I can't find the right words to convey how I am feeling.

I have come to realize, however, that no person can help me feel better if I don't make the right choices. I have to tell myself, *God has called me to a life beyond my fear and anxiety, so I am not going to live trapped in darkness anymore. I am going to pick myself up and trust that God will give me a sound mind, as the Scriptures promise.*

With God's help, I use his Word like a razor blade. I scrape away the thick soot that the enemy is using to steal my light. I am like Jude. I will live in God's love, God's *perfect* love.

> *Loving Lord,*
> *Thank you for your perfect love, which casts out fear.*
> *Thank you for the Scriptures you have placed in my*
> *heart and on my lips. I will use your truth to shut*
> *the mouth of the father of lies. Please continue to*
> *teach me that you are my help when the weight of*
> *depression, anxiety, panic, and despair begins to*
> *crush me. I can stand on this truth: You have not*
> *given me a spirit of fear, but of power and of love*
> *and of a sound mind. May I and all single moms*
> *walk in this truth today. Let us speak this truth over*
> *our children. May our lights shine on them so that*
> *our families will not be shrouded in hopelessness. I*
> *pray that we remain in your perfect love.*
>
> > *In your light-giving name,*
> > *Amen.*

43

Making Small Blessings Add Up

Make sure that your character is free from the love of
money, being content with what you have.

Hebrews 13:5 NASB

This morning, did your own private robot roll into your bedroom
and wake you up by playing some of your favorite songs on his
onboard, high-tech sound system?

Did a famous TV chef cook your breakfast?

The last time you took a trip, did you travel by private jet or
stretch limousine?

For me and every single mom I know, the answer to all these
questions is an emphatic *no!* (Or "I wish!") But life doesn't need
a lot of fancy and expensive stuff to be amazing. Really. Every day,
God provides dozens of small blessings, blessings that anyone
can enjoy if they just have the eyes to see them and the hearts to
appreciate them. My single-mom friends and I have been trying
to cultivate more gratitude into our lives. It's amazing the blessings you can enjoy when you take the time to appreciate them.

The warmth of that special someone's smile. Watching a favorite TV show or movie with a couple of close friends. The beauty
of a sunset. Hearing "Great work!" from a boss or coworker. The
comfort of crawling into bed after a busy, busy day. The hug of
a child.

Always remember that enjoying God's small blessings can make a so-called common life uncommonly good. The difference between an ordinary life and an *extra*ordinary one is the *extra* care we take to appreciate all the ways God shows he cares for us.

"God's gifts put man's best dreams to shame."
—Elizabeth Barrett Browning

44

Let's Get Personal

Behold what manner of love the Father has bestowed on
us, that we should be called children of God!

1 John 3:1 NKJV

A huge gap, a Grand Canyon, stands between knowing about God and truly *knowing* him. For many of us, God is like a movie. We've read the reviews, seen the previews. We can summarize the plot, even quote a line or two of dialogue. We can even form a thumbs-up or thumbs-down opinion. But we haven't actually seen the whole picture.

Or God is like an exotic vacation destination...out there somewhere. We've seen the brochures, maybe even watched some video on a promotional website. The place sure looks great. But we've never been there.

God is your loving Creator, and he wants you to experience him firsthand. So read his book. Listen to his music. Hear his modern-day "prophets" (pastors, youth pastors, singers, authors, and musicians).

Take time to simply be still in God's presence and ask him to fill your head and your heart with his love.

Further, don't let your prayers become obligatory quick monologues to God. Or long wish lists. Make them conversations with him.

To have a close, rewarding relationship with God, you don't have to be perfect. But you do need to be genuinely committed to the relationship. Just as a woman can't be "mostly married" or "somewhat pregnant," you cannot have a "sort of" relationship with God. A relationship with the all-loving, all-powerful God of the universe just doesn't work that way. Being close to God includes spending time with him at his house, with his people. Making time to worship. Time to praise. Time to support and be supported by other believers.

We single moms are so busy that we are tempted to steal some extra me-time by skipping church, Bible study, or small-group time. But these things feed us more than we realize. Time with God and his people can *be* me-time!

If you avoid church or let your Bible gather dust on a shelf, will God still love you? Of course. He loved you long before you were even aware of him. He loved you before the first church was built or the first word of the Bible was penned. But if you truly want to grow close to God, to return even a portion of the love he has showered on you, you need to spend time with him. Why not start today?

> *"All difficulties in prayer can be traced to one cause: praying as if God were absent."*
>
> —Teresa of Avila

45

Revealing Your True Beauty

You created my inmost being;
you knit me together in my mother's womb.
I praise you because I am fearfully
and wonderfully made;
your works are wonderful,
I know that full well.
My frame was not hidden from you
when I was made in the secret place,
when I was woven together in the depths of the earth.
Your eyes saw my unformed body;
all the days ordained for me were written in your book
before one of them came to be.

Psalm 139: 13-16

If you've recently stepped on the scale and cringed at the numbers, perhaps you should consider moving to Mauritania. People in this West African country believe that the more a woman weighs, the better her chance of securing a husband.

Meanwhile, along the borders of Thailand and Burma, a long neck is considered attractive. A really, really long neck. Women begin this "beauty treatment" as young girls by stacking more and more heavy metal bands around their necks. By the time they reach adulthood, these women have weakened the muscles in their elongated necks so much that if they removed the bands, they would suffocate.

In Ethiopia, scars are cut into a woman's stomach to enhance her beauty.

The Maori women of New Zealand cover their lips and chins with blue tattoos.

One might think that American beauty standards are more reasonable, but even those standards have shifted dramatically. In the 1700s, pear-shaped hips were considered attractive. (So was shaving your eyebrows and replacing them with ones made of press-on mouse skin!)

In the 1800s, women were encouraged to look frail and pale. In the 1920s, women bound their chests to have more boyish figures.

When it comes to measuring one's worth, appearance is always part of the equation. And for centuries, women (and men too) have gone to extremes to meet the current standards of beauty. In some cases, even that is not enough. Some women just have to rise *above* the current standard. They demand the biggest breasts, the tightest abs, and the best hair.

In reality, each person is like a single piece in a giant jigsaw puzzle that stretches through time. We all have our own shapes and colors, each one of us filling a unique spot that helps complete the final picture. Beauty comes in all ages, colors, and shapes.

You may be an eye-catching flower petal on a begonia, a burst of lava from an erupting volcano, or a gleaming tooth on a Bengal tiger.

Or you may be a piece of blue sky. You know, the ones that at first glance all seem to look alike. But try to put one piece of sky into the spot designed for another piece, and what happens? It won't fit.

You can try jamming it in, pounding it down, or bending the corners up a bit. But even if you succeed in forcing that piece into a spot where it doesn't belong, it will never look quite right. And somewhere else in the puzzle there will be a hole in the picture—a spot where that now-mangled piece would have fit just perfectly.

Every piece plays its part. And every person plays her part. Sometimes it takes a while to find your part, your special spot. That's part of the adventure of being a woman. That's part of the adventure of being a single mom. No matter your age, you're still discovering who you are and where you fit—what part of the big picture you were created to fill. That process involves trial and error, just like working any puzzle with dozens and dozens of pieces. That means you can feel free to try out for the community theater, see if playing guitar is your thing, or start writing a blog. You can go back to school to earn that degree you've always craved.

You can feel equally proud of being a juggler, a fiber artist, a budding musician, a beat poet, or a humor writer.

If you're searching for a standard by which to measure yourself, forget about comparing yourself against others—physically or any other way. Every time you compare yourself with another piece of the puzzle, you lose sight of how truly valuable that one-of-a-kind *you* really is. You lose sight of your true worth.

It's like comparing limes to lemons or blue sky to blue sea. Mountain air to sea air. Redwood trees to Sequoia trees.

If you must compare, compare who you are *trying* to be with who you believe you truly are in your heart and soul. If something is off there, pray that God will get you back on the right path.

Remember, no one can ever be a better you than *you*.

Creator God,
Thank you for caring about my inmost being. Let me never fail to be grateful for the fact that I am fearfully and wonderfully made. I have a purpose, and I know you will provide all that I need to fulfill that purpose. I am a valuable child because I am your child.

I praise you and thank you.

Amen.

46

What Really Matters?

As Jesus and his disciples were on their way, he came
to a village where a woman named Martha opened her
home to him. She had a sister called Mary, who sat at
the Lord's feet listening to what he said. But Martha was
distracted by all the preparations that had to be made.
She came to him and asked, "Lord, don't you care that
my sister has left me to do the work by myself? Tell her
to help me!" "Martha, Martha," the Lord answered, "you
are worried and upset about many things, but few things
are needed—or indeed only one. Mary has chosen what
is better, and it will not be taken away from her."

Luke 10:38-42

I can't count the times I have heard the story of Mary and Martha. When I talk with my friends about it, it's interesting to see who identifies with Mary and who relates more to Martha. As you might guess from what you have read in this book, I totally identify with Martha. That makes this Scripture passage difficult for me to read.

Like Martha, when I entertain guests in my home, I always strive to make everything just right. I want the house to look spotless, the food to taste delicious, and each guest to feel welcome and appreciated.

Whenever I think about this story, I have to remind myself that Jesus truly appreciated Martha's efforts to make things special for her guests. He understood her personality. She was a busy bee and a perfectionist, just like yours truly. That's why Martha clashed with her sister.

Jesus recognized a teachable moment in the conflict. He sensed Martha's stress, so he assured her, communicating that everything didn't have to be perfect. He wanted her to understand that she had a rare opportunity to spend time in the presence of God's Son. I can just hear him saying to her, "My daughter, my beloved daughter, just be with me for a while. Choose me, not the distractions and busywork. Just rest in my presence and be still."

Given all the busyness of life, I need to combat my "Martha tendencies" and lean in to Mary's approach. I need to stop working so hard and ask myself, *Do I really need to obsess over my to-do list right now? Is that what truly matters?*

If I answer these questions honestly, I will realize that what I really need to do is take some quiet time to be alone with the Lord. I need to sit at his feet and meet his eyes with mine—before all the busyness kicks in. I need to carve out time with the Lord first, because that will set the tone for whatever comes next. That's why I strive to spend time with Jesus before I start the housework, before I make breakfast for my kids and help them get ready for school.

When I give the Lord my undivided attention, he gives me the strength and the energy to face the day ahead and complete the work set before me. In fact, I have learned that I need that time of stillness to focus and gather myself.

Sometimes, my boys interrupt my quiet times, but they are learning that "Mom's time with the Lord" is crucial and that they need to give me space unless there's something that truly cannot wait.

I hope I am leading them by example. I hope they will adopt a similar practice in their lives. That's what happened with me. My mom and dad modeled the practice of God's presence *every single day*. I recall waking up in the morning and seeing them in their designated chairs, enjoying their morning devotions. They started their days, quietly and reverently, with the Lord. Occasionally they would talk together afterward, sharing what the Lord had taught them.

I visit my mom and dad as often as I can, and I am happy to report that they are still doing their daily devotions after all these years. What an example they are for their adult children and their grandchildren.

Heavenly Father,
Thank you for being the ultimate teacher. I am so thankful you that you are gentle with us, showing us, in such a loving way, how to live this life. I want to learn to focus on what really matters, and that is you. I confess that so many times, I am like Martha. I want things to be just right, and I feel so busy and overwhelmed as a result. I need to set aside time to sit at your feet and bask in your presence. Please give me the energy and the strength to

get done what needs to get done. I want to be an example to my children. I want them to see that when I put you first, you allow me to accomplish all that I need to do.

I love you, my Lord. I pray these things in your name.

Amen.

47

Revealing Our True Value

We have this treasure in jars of clay to show that this all-surpassing power is from God and not from us. We are hard pressed on every side, but not crushed; perplexed, but not in despair; persecuted, but not abandoned; struck down, but not destroyed.

2 Corinthians 4:7-9

*E*very now and then, a new TV commercial appears, trumpeting the virtues of the latest technology in nonstick cookware. Who knew that a simple frying pan could be "revolutionary"? According to the ads, some of today's pots and pans are so advanced, someone could cook glue in them and even *that* wouldn't stick.

Some people are like these miracle pans. Nothing seems to stick to them. No sadness. No insult. No mistake. No career setback. They seem impervious to everything.

Many of us single moms, however, find that *everything* sticks. The shame. The disappointment. The sense of hopelessness. We try to get rid of that annoying crud, but it won't be scrubbed away, even with vigorous effort and industrial-strength cleansers.

That is where God comes in. We don't have to be spotless for him. We don't have to pretend, *Nothing is wrong here! Nothing bad is sticking to me!*

God meets us where we are. We don't have to get to a certain point on our spiritual path before he will show up.

Yes, he meets us where we are—and *as* we are. With all the dried-on sin and shame and insecurity. With all the scratches and scars, dings and dents.

Perhaps the apostle Paul said it best in the Scripture above: "We have this treasure in jars of clay." Let's never miss the importance of this imagery. Paul said jars of *clay*, not pure gold. Not space-age alloys. Let's face it—we are not the most amazing containers on the market. But inside we hold treasure.

May the brilliance and power of the treasure we hold inside us give us purpose and love...regardless of what might be sticking to us on the outside.

> *Dear God,*
> *When I look in the mirror or compare myself with women I know, especially the happily married women, I can feel inadequate. May I never forget the light inside of me. Let me treasure the precious Spirit who comforts and guides me. Thank you for making me worthy to carry such a gift with me everywhere I go.*
>
> *In your name,*
> *Amen.*

48

Making the Ordinary Extraordinary

Store up for yourselves treasures in heaven, where moths and vermin do not destroy, and where thieves do not break in and steal. For where your treasure is, there your heart will be also.

Matthew 6:20-21

*H*as this ever happened to you?

You've folded the last T-shirt, paid the last bill, or answered the last email. But then, instead of mentally checking another task off your to-do list or shaking your head at the monotony of daily life, you smile. You lean back and breathe deeply. You feel satisfied, centered.

True, you haven't cured any disease or solved world hunger, but you've done something well. You have made your home (your life!) more organized and more efficient. *Better.* And for this, it's good to thank God.

You see, in the common tasks of everyday life, we can find ourselves at our most focused, disciplined, and poised. We work with no ulterior motives. This is all about keeping one's life moving forward, not veering off into the weeds. This is about bringing skill and dedication and yes, love, to the mundane. In the process, we transform the mundane into the meaningful.

Do you *love* every one of your daily tasks? Probably not. But can you do every task with love—love for a friend, a child, and life itself? Yes. Can you do it with love for the God who makes it all possible?

Yes. Most definitely, yes.

When we are present in the everyday moments, we find that God is present with us. And where God is, the flicker of a holy flame can help us see the commonplace in a whole new light.

> *"Love stretches your heart and*
> *makes you big inside."*
>
> —Margaret Walker

49

Who Validates You?

It is fine to be zealous, provided the purpose is good.
Galatians 4:18

*D*on't be so obsessed about other people's opinion of you! Why do you care so much what other people think?"

As kids, how many of us heard this advice from our parents as we struggled to fit in with friends on the block or peers at school or youth group? Like a lot of parental guidance, this counsel packs a lot of merit. The most well-adjusted people I know are those who understand that their happiness does not depend on others' opinions. They know happiness is an inside job. They trust their knowledge, insights, and instincts. Their God-given sense of purpose. They allow themselves to evolve naturally rather than be manipulated by others like pawns on a chessboard.

Whether you are choosing a career path or assessing your readiness for a serious romantic relationship, it's vital to trust yourself. That doesn't mean ignoring advice or guidance from the wise people in your life, but it does mean not being *controlled* by those outside voices. People have chosen the wrong major or the wrong career (or even married the right person at the wrong time) because they let extraneous voices drown out the one inside. And if something feels wrong, feels too soon or too risky, it probably is. Maybe God's Spirit is trying to tell you something.

Maybe you need to search the Scriptures or share your concerns with a pastor, counselor, or trusted friend. But in the end, you must own your decisions. You need to be able to face God with clear eyes and a pure motive.

If you tend to be a people pleaser, try to stop looking outside yourself for validation and approval—in essence, letting others define your happiness. Take care of yourself on the inside. Trust God and let that divine inner light illuminate your life's path.

> *Heavenly Father,*
> *Your Word declares that you have plans to prosper*
> *me, not harm me. You created a plan to give me*
> *a hope and a future. People might disappoint me*
> *with their words and deeds, but not you. You have*
> *divinely appointed me. You have divinely validated*
> *me. Others might give up on me, but you never*
> *will. Let me take hold of these truths through faith*
> *in Christ Jesus.*
>
> *In your name,*
> *Amen.*

50

Let's Be Passionate About Compassion

Remember also those being mistreated,
as though you felt their pain in your own bodies.

Hebrews 13:3 NLT

*W*hen I start feeling down or discouraged, I find that I am encouraged by stories of strong and faithful women. You're about to read about one such woman, one of my heroes.

Of the many great figures in American history, few are as admirable as Clara Barton. She began her career as a teacher at age fifteen. *Fifteen!* Take a moment to let that sink in. And this was in 1836, when almost all teachers were men. (And certainly not *teenage* men.)

Later in life, in her forties, she served as a nurse in the Civil War, sometimes risking her life in the heat of battle to tend to the wounded. Her courage, expertise, and grace earned her the title "Angel of the Battlefield." She didn't just tend to soldiers' wounds. She read to them, wrote letters for them, and listened to their concerns and stories. And she prayed with them.

After the war ended, she worked to reunite injured soldiers with their families.

At age 60, she founded the American Red Cross, which she led for 23 years, never drawing a salary.

At this point, you might be wondering, What was Clara Barton's secret for success? How was she able to serve others so well? You might be surprised to learn that her secret is a quality you possess, one you can build upon.

The hallmark of Barton's life was compassion. This word comes from the Latin stems *com* (with) and *pati* (suffer). Compassionate people suffer with others. They take others' pain and grief as their own.

Barton displayed her compassion at an early age. When she was 11, her older brother David was building a barn but fell from the rafters and was seriously injured. For two years, Clara helped care for David, developing the skills and patience that would serve her on the battlefield many years later.

Even though she worked on some of the Civil War's bloodiest battlefields, she didn't feel that her service was anything extraordinary. "While our soldiers can stand and fight," she said matter-of-factly, "I can stand and feed and nurse them. You must never so much as think if you like it or not, if it is bearable or not. You must never think of anything but the need and how to meet it."

We can't all serve on the battlefield or start huge benevolent organizations. But we can all be like Clara Barton by being compassionate people who see needs and try our best to meet them. We can live out the words of one of my favorite verses: "Never walk away from someone who deserves help; your hand is *God's* hand for that person" (Proverbs 3:27 MSG).

*"Would that Christ would teach my
soul a prayer that would plead to the
Father for grace sufficient for you."*

—Clara Barton

51

Present Company Accepted

May the God who gives endurance and encouragement
give you the same attitude of mind toward each other
that Christ Jesus had, so that with one mind and one
voice you may glorify the God and Father of our Lord
Jesus Christ. Accept one another, then, just as Christ
accepted you, in order to bring praise to God.
Romans 15:5-7

*I*f someone asked you, "Who are you?" how would you respond?
Some people define themselves by their lineage, their job title, their
bank account balance, their social-media presence, or the carefully
maintained image they see in the mirror before going out in public.

But none of those things captures a person's true essence. And
all of them can lead to a fundamental dissatisfaction with life—
the continual striving for a more prestigious job title, a fatter
bank account, or a more appealing reflection in the mirror.

Every New Year, millions of people make resolutions related
to self-improvement. But what if the next time January 1 rolls
around, you resolve to simply accept yourself as God made you?
To acknowledge that yes, you have faults, but you are still a good
person. A generous person. A good friend, a hardworking and
responsible single mother. A loyal sibling or friend. A beloved child
of God. Someone who does way more good than harm every day.

Accepting yourself doesn't mean you become complacent or refuse to grow as a person. Instead, it means you appreciate your own value—and that value becomes the catalyst for self-improvement. It's positive reinforcement rather than negative reinforcement.

Those who have studied self-esteem have found that people who accept themselves can take defeat and disappointment in stride rather than letting it destroy them. They refuse to be defined by life's inevitable failures. They see them merely as obstacles to climb over. Conversely, unhappy people make a practice of magnifying each defeat to monstrous proportions. They identify with each failure. They believe the failure is a sign of more to come. Instead of thinking, *I fell short of my goal this time*, they tell themselves, *I AM a failure; I'll always be a failure*.

Think of the close friends or family members in your life. These people aren't perfect. They've made mistakes, they've faltered in their paths from time to time, and they've probably even hurt you somewhere along the road. But you still accept them and value them. Shouldn't you do the same for yourself?

> *"One of the greatest moments in anybody's developing experience is when he no longer tries to hide from himself but determines to get acquainted with himself as he really is."*
> —Norman Vincent Peale

52

Our God Honors Sincere Effort

Laugh with your happy friends when they're happy; share
tears when they're down. Get along with each other; don't
be stuck-up. Make friends with nobodies; don't be the
great somebody.
Romans 12:15-16 MSG

I heard about a single mom who, after weeks of effort, finally
convinced her teen daughter to accompany her to church in their
small farming community. As the pastor stood at the pulpit and
began his sermon, the teen thought, *This guy is the worst preacher
I've ever heard. He isn't as funny as my teachers or people on YouTube.
He doesn't have a very good speaking voice. And he looks nervous and
uncomfortable up there.*

The girl sat bored and discouraged for the next 20 minutes,
wishing her mother had let her bring the smartphone—or better yet, stay home and sleep in. She sighed with relief when she
heard the words "And in conclusion…"

Thank goodness that's over, she thought cynically. Then she
heard a faint sniffling sound and turned to a woman sitting next
to her. The woman was sobbing quietly and dabbing her eyes
with a tattered tissue. "That was just what I needed to hear," she
said, her voice ringing with gratitude and sincerity.

The teen's mom nodded sympathetically and gave the woman a fresh tissue from her purse.

The teen swallowed hard, feeling a bit guilty. But she learned a valuable lesson that day: Through God's grace and provision, a message that might lack in style can still speak to the hearts of listeners.

Have you ever been afraid to write a poem, draw a picture, crochet a cap, give a speech, or sing a song because you think your talents aren't worthy of anyone's attention? If so, take heart. God doesn't expect your endeavors to be polished and perfect. He's not going to rate your efforts against someone else's. He simply expects you to be sincere and faithful. And if you do your best, your efforts can touch hearts.

It's substance, not style, that will make your labors of love helpful.

"Every calling is great when greatly pursued."
—Oliver Wendell Holmes

53

Jesus's "One" Wish

Every kingdom divided against itself is brought to desolation, and every city or house divided against itself will not stand.

Matthew 12:25 NKJV

*J*esus's last formal prayer before he died on the cross was for unity within the body of Christ. As he awaited the most terrible ordeal imaginable, Jesus took the time to pray for all believers: "I pray also for those who will believe in me...that all of them may be one...that they may be brought to complete unity" (John 17:20-23).

Sadly, today that body has been wounded and disjointed—not so much from outside assaults but by quarrels from within.

Churches split and splinter with regularity. And many authors and artists are attacked for their alleged incorrect beliefs and motives. People are judged by which politician they support or fail to support.

All the while, the world that Christians are called to witness to is watching.

Think about your life. Are there religious cliques in your neighborhood—even within your church? Have you found yourself being criticized for the kind of music you listen to ("Hip-hop can't possibly be Christian!"), the denomination you belong to, or the TV shows you watch? If you are a single mom because of divorce, have people taken sides with you or your ex? More important, have *you* taken sides? If you are a single woman who has chosen to adopt, have people judged you for not seeking a husband?

Imagine the impact Christians could have on the world if we quit fighting among ourselves.

Want to help bring about unity and make a difference in the lives of those around you? Here are a few suggestions:

1. Be humble and encourage humility in others. Humility is a wellspring of Christian unity. As Philippians 2:3 teaches, "In humility value others above yourselves."

2. Don't label people. Labels demean. Labels limit. Labels reduce complex human beings to stereotypes. They stifle opportunities for fellowship, they blind us to the good in others, and they emphasize differences rather than common ground.

3. Avoid gossip. Gossip has destroyed friendships, fueled feuds, and even shattered entire churches. Gossip is tempting. To help resist the temptation, keep in mind that the Bible says the Lord *hates* a person who stirs up dissension among fellow believers (Proverbs 6:19).

For Christians to effectively witness to a lost world, we must stop fighting among ourselves. You can't pull a truck out of a ditch with one tiny thread—or even hundreds of individual threads.

However, if you weave the threads together, they can become a rope that is strong enough for the task.

In the same manner, it's time for Christians to lay aside their differences, join forces, and pull together.

> *Dear Lord,*
> *It is so significant to me that Jesus prayed for unity even while facing the pain and humiliation of the cross. Help me to remember (and to model) the fact that fingers pointed in criticism and judgment would be put to better use being folded in prayer for togetherness and unity. Or reaching out to help someone in need regardless of his or her denomination, political affiliation, ethnic heritage, or anything else.*
> *In your loving name,*
> *Amen.*

54

The Fear of Falling

I lift up my eyes to the mountains—
where does my help come from?
My help comes from the LORD,
the Maker of heaven and earth.
He will not let your foot slip—
he who watches over you will not slumber;
indeed, he who watches over Israel
will neither slumber nor sleep.
The LORD watches over you—
the LORD is your shade at your right hand;
the sun will not harm you by day,
nor the moon by night.

Psalm 121:1-6

*L*ike a lot of Coloradans, I love being active in the mountains—skiing, hiking, and rock climbing. I really love to climb. When the mountains are encased in snow and ice, you can find me at an indoor climbing wall, challenging myself and schooling any guys who might think they can compete with me. (Just sayin'.)

Katie Brown is also from Colorado (Golden, Colorado, to be specific), and I look up to her...even though she's barely 5 feet tall and weighs only 95 pounds. You see, she stands a lot taller once she's nimbly scaled a 100-foot climbing wall (that's equivalent to a 10-story building). Katie is a "difficulty climber"—in fact, she's a world champion and multiple gold medalist at the X Games.

As you might imagine, it's intimidating for a small person to attack climbing walls and cliffs that are 20 times her height. But Katie says that extreme faith can bring her peace even in extremely dangerous challenges.

> I know that I couldn't have done what I've done without being a Christian. My faith in God doesn't get rid of my healthy fear of climbing extreme heights, but it does help me deal with it. It takes away a lot of the pressure, because you know that God's not going to condemn you if you don't win. So there's nothing to worry about. When I see others competing, I wonder how I could compete if I didn't have faith in God.[3]

The walls in your life might not be literal, physical cliffs. They might be emotional, relational, or spiritual. And it's okay to feel intimidated or frightened by the walls in your life. As Katie notes, it would be unhealthy *not* to appreciate their significance.

But like Katie, you can rest secure in the truth that God will not condemn you if you can't get to the top of your wall—or if it takes you hundreds of attempts. God is more concerned in your faithful effort. So climb on.

> *"If we will only attempt to walk toward God,*
> *he is pleased even with our stumbles."*
>
> —C.S. Lewis

55

Travel Light, Travel Right

The world and its desires pass away,
but whoever does the will of God lives forever.
1 John 2:17

What's on your wish list right now? What do you wish you had but don't possess? For many, money and material possessions top the list. Americans have a possession obsession—we want bigger and better TVs, faster computers, smarter smartphones, and trendier tablets with more memory and longer battery life.

For others, status and success are the ultimate prizes. Some want to be the next pop star or game-show champion. Others hope for a prettier face or a better body.

Seeking "the good life" isn't inherently bad—as long as this quest is secondary to "the God life." Unfortunately, material possessions and physical attractiveness can become all-consuming goals, and we can be driven to fulfill shallow, self-gratifying obsessions with no eternal significance.

God's Word teaches us to travel light. In fact, Jesus instructed his followers to take with them only the bare necessities when they set out on a journey. He reminded them not to be distracted by the glitter of money or the aura of fame and power. Even when his life was at stake, his focus was clear: "My kingdom is not of this world."

In talking with some of my fellow single moms, I have realized that one of the silver linings to the dark cloud of divorce and family upheaval is the discovery of how much *stuff* a family can accumulate—and how much of it is unnecessary. Much of what we buy, what we own, doesn't really make our lives better. It just takes up space.

In truth, the light of God's divine love is so brilliant that it makes everything else dull in comparison. God's light is what we should run to because only in that light can we find true happiness and fulfillment. So don't misplace your hope in things that don't last or that have no eternal value. Put "loving and serving God" atop your list of life's priorities. Because life has treasures to offer, but God tops them all.

> *Dear Provider God,*
>
> *Thank you for all you have given me. I am beyond fortunate, especially when I compare my lifestyle to that of people in other countries or even parts of my own state. Please help me value my spiritual gifts and blessings more than anything in the material world. Help me keep my "stuff" in perspective. And if I need to give up certain possessions, I ask for the strength to do just that.*
>
> *In your name,*
> *Amen.*

56

Inside Every "Don't" Is a "Do"

Your word is a lamp for my feet,
a light on my path.
I have taken an oath and confirmed it,
that I will follow your righteous laws.
I have suffered much;
preserve my life, LORD, according to your word.
Psalm 119:105-107

Why did God give us lists of rules to follow? Why does the Bible so often say, "Thou shalt not _____"?

Is God some kind of egomaniac who created people just so he would have somebody to push around? Wouldn't life be simpler without all the commandments?

Look at it this way: Why doesn't a mother let her toddler touch a hot stove? Why doesn't she let her kid run out into traffic? Why does a doctor insist on having a patient's medical history before prescribing medication? In each of these examples, the rules might not make sense (and might even prove quite frustrating) to the person required to obey them.

A toddler wants to touch the stove because the orange glow is alluring. A child wants to play on the street because being confined to the yard is boring. And a sick person wants medication "right now." The background check is just more red tape, another roadblock on the path to healing. When each of these people collides with a brick wall of rules, the first reaction is often to find a way around, over, under, or through that troublesome wall.

Little thought is given to the fact that the rules are meant to protect, to ensure safety and happiness.

Similarly, abiding by our Creator's commandments ensures our protection, fulfillment, peace, and well-being. The quality of our lives is a product of our choices, and we don't always have the information, wisdom, or perspective to make the best decisions. That's precisely why the God who loves us and yearns to see us succeed has given us rules to live by.

At their core, even the commandments that begin with "Don't" or "Thou shalt not" are positive. For example, "Don't covet" is another way of saying *do* appreciate what you have. Be grateful for it. Get true joy from it by avoiding comparing your stuff with someone else's.

"Don't kill" means *do* value and treasure life—yours and that of others. Realize that God created every person with the capacity to do good in the world. Be aware of the evil inherent in maliciously robbing another human being of his or her life. Of potential. Of dreams.

"Thou shalt not steal" is another way of saying you *shall* respect others' property. If you need more possessions, more money, or more whatever, go out and earn it.

If you have been viewing the Ten Commandments or other biblical rules as big sticks God uses to beat his creation into submission, it's time to shift your perspective. God is for you, not against you.

This is a truth I am trying to instill in my two boys and in myself.

Wise Father God,

How blessed we are to have a sovereign Lord who cares enough about us to provide rules to help us achieve the abundant life Jesus promised. May we all look at your commandments in a more positive light. Thank you for being for us, not against us.

In your name,

Amen.

57

Putting Proof into Promises

I seek you with all my heart;
do not let me stray from your commands.
I have hidden your word in my heart
that I might not sin against you.
Praise be to you, LORD;
teach me your decrees.
Psalm 119:10-12

*T*hink about the last time you heard a politician make a promise. What was your reaction? An eye-roll? A weary sigh? Maybe a sarcastic "Yeah, *right!*"

Yes, at this point in the twenty-first century, promises and oaths are not what they used to be. We've been burned too many times. We've seen that words, no matter how sincerely and loudly they are uttered, can be hollow.

Your manager or your mayor says, "I promise."

You counter, "Prove it."

No wonder God's promises stand out from the crowd. They have substance. It's certainly no accident that so many of God's promises have been accompanied by tangible and memorable signs and wonders. Moses's burning bush. Aaron's rod that budded. David's five smooth stones. And let's not forget the rainbows—thousands of years' worth of rainbows.

When God declares allegiance to us, he shows us he means it. The God who loves us is the same one who sets the stars in the night sky and who follows winter with spring and night with day. As Scripture says, "The heavens declare the glory of God; the skies proclaim the work of his hands" (Psalm 19:1).

If only we will open our eyes, we will see all around us proclamations of God's might and declarations of his love.

Some Christians today observe seven sacraments (baptism, Eucharist, confirmation, reconciliation, anointing of the sick, marriage, and ordination). Others recognize only two. And still other believers simply are not into what they call "that whole sacrament thing."

Maybe we are all wrong.

Whatever we may choose to call them, there are hundreds of signs of God's faithfulness. Hundreds of things that can be sacramental—worthy of holy awe—if seen through holy eyes.

May you see God's faithfulness in myriad ways and shapes. The comforting hug from a loved one. The smile on your child's face. The melody of a favorite hymn. Even the pages of a book. And remember always that *how* God shows his love is not as important as the life-saving fact that God *does* love. That's a promise we can always count on. That's a promise with proof.

> *"It is not the magnitude of our actions but the amount of love that is put into them that matters."*
>
> —Mother Teresa

58

Finding Lost Perspective

Do not worry about your life, what you will eat or drink; or
about your body, what you will wear. Is not life more than
food, and the body more than clothes? Look at the birds
of the air; they do not sow or reap or store away in barns,
and yet your heavenly Father feeds them. Are you not
much more valuable than they? Can any one of you by
worrying add a single hour to your life?

Matthew 6:25-27

It's amazing how minor irritations can take a single mom's eyes
off God. Tension headaches interrupt our sleep. Telemarketers
interrupt our dinner time. Corporate restructurings interrupt
our career progress. Workplace emergencies interrupt our vaca-
tions. And to be fair, troubles on the home front often interrupt
us at work. I don't know about you, but when I get a call from
the school, it's usually not to inform me, "Everything went perfectly in every class today, and your son had absolutely no problems. Didn't get sick at lunch. Didn't get bullied. Didn't forget
his homework. Just thought you should know—have a nice day!"

When we get a case of *Life Interrupted*, we must step back
and try to regain our perspective. Will the world stop turning if
we don't quite make that project deadline? Will babies no longer smile and blackbirds no longer sing if we can't do absolutely

everything we want while on vacation? Will our job become less meaningful if a less-deserving person is named associate of the month?

When we look at life clearly, what is a traffic ticket or flat tire or flight delay compared to being loved wholly and eternally by Almighty God? What can possibly compare to being made clean from all our sins? Even when life is hard, life is still good. Because our God is *good*.

> *"The Lord stands above the new day, for*
> *God has made it. All restlessness, all*
> *worry and anxiety flee before him."*
>
> —Dietrich Bonhoeffer

59

Let's Get Real

The LORD detests dishonest scales,
but accurate weights find favor with him.
When pride comes, then comes disgrace,
but with humility comes wisdom.
The integrity of the upright guides them,
but the unfaithful are destroyed by their duplicity.
Wealth is worthless in the day of wrath,
but righteousness delivers from death.
The righteousness of the blameless
makes their paths straight,
but the wicked are brought down by their own wickedness.
The righteousness of the upright delivers them,
but the unfaithful are trapped by evil desires.
Proverbs 11:1-6

*A*s an artist, I regard people like Jamie Martin as heroes. You have probably never heard of him, but he's one of the best art detectives in the world. Recently, he helped uncover an $80 million art scam, the largest in American history. Martin describes his one-person company, Orion Analytical, as a "microniche materials analysis and consulting firm." (See why I prefer "art detective"?)

Martin's work on the record-breaking art scam included revealing 40 forgeries created by a Chinese artist in Queens,

New York. Remarkably, this scammer was able to create dozens of forgeries that were sold or consigned by Manhattan's prestigious Knoedler Gallery between 1994 and 2008. This endeavor fooled several curators, art historians, law-enforcement officials, and other art experts.

Martin combines his vast knowledge of art history with science to uncover deception. For example, he examined a purported Jackson Pollock painting and used 3-D images from a stereomicroscope to reveal that Pollock's signature was traced with a needle. He also used a high-tech Raman microscope to identify the presence of Red 170, a pigment that was virtually nonexistent until decades after Pollock's death in 1956. (The Raman can analyze sample areas as small as one-thousandth of a millimeter.)

When he takes on a case, Martin begins by asking questions: Did the forger paint over another painting? Are the materials used consistent with the era? Were some elements added later? Is the signature real? In one case, Martin examined a 12-foot-square painting that was supposedly created in 1932. The paints and the canvas used were consistent with the era, but he found a single polypropylene fiber from the forger's clothing embedded in the paint. This synthetic fiber wasn't created until 1958.

Because of his expertise, Martin is often brought in as an expert witness in art fraud cases or as a trainer for the FBI and other law-enforcement agencies. "As a scientist," he explains, "I feel a responsibility to preserve art history so that future generations have an accurate, rich understanding of who these artists were and what they created."[4]

Martin's story reminds me of a sermon illustration I heard a long time ago.

A man who thought he had an amazing replica of a Leonardo da Vinci painting took his work of art to a museum. He showed the copied painting to the curator to get her reaction.

To the man's surprise, the curator immediately identified the painting as a fake. Then she went on to name the copyist, his nationality, and the likely date of the painting's creation.

"But how could you know all that so quickly?" the man sputtered. "I have seen pictures of the da Vinci original, and this likeness seems really, really good to me."

The curator smiled. "People who make a living copying the masters have little imagination of their own," she explained. "This painter's particular choice of subject, brush strokes, and areas of color emphasis practically scream 'Copy!' Think of those celebrity impersonators you see on TV. You know how they overemphasize vocal inflections, catchphrases, and gestures? It's the same thing with people who impersonate painters."

As a single mom, here is what stories like this mean to me. We are blessed with a wide variety of inspirational role models—businesswomen, athletes, artists, entertainers, and more. But this blessing can backfire on us. If we want to distinguish ourselves, we need to be innovators, not imitators. It is great to gain inspiration from someone we admire, but we should be inspired to develop our own distinctive styles.

My first book (also published by Harvest House) is titled *Faith Outside the Lines: More Than Just a Journal for the Creative Believer*. It was somewhat scary to create that book because it isn't easy to define. It's part journal, part activity book, and part art primer. It was a risk for me and my publisher, but it's authentically "me." That was my goal—in that book and in this one.

I encourage you to follow your own path as well and to let the results rest in God's hands. The world does not need clones of established bestselling authors. They are doing their thing, and may God bless them. The world doesn't need clones of successful power-women either. It needs the one and only YOU!

Unique heavenly Father,
In this age when failure is more public than ever, it's tempting to play things safe and follow the crowd. To be a copy of what's acceptable rather than to be an original. In my times of uncertainty, lead me to live my version of life, not someone else's. It's okay if my life doesn't look like everyone else's. It's okay if my kids aren't like everyone else's either. Inspire me to focus on what I do well. When I fake it, I fool almost no one—especially not you. Please give me the gift of authenticity.

In your name,
Amen.

60

Who Wants to Be Happy?
Any Volunteers?

Whatever you give is acceptable if you give it eagerly.
And give according to what you have,
not what you don't have.
2 Corinthians 8:12 NLT

*T*he mere mention of the word "volunteer" makes some people uncomfortable, if not exhausted. Given the overcrowded lives most of us face, who has the time or energy to volunteer? Many of my single-mom friends and I really struggle with this challenge. Discretionary time is a precious commodity, and most of us are trying to trim our to-do lists, not add to them.

The trouble with such rationales is that volunteering is the right thing to do, and there aren't enough people to do it. Most likely, your community is overflowing with needs. Libraries need reading tutors. Thrift stores yearn for volunteer cashiers. Churches crave Sunday school teachers. Soup kitchens need servers.

Just the other day, a friend posted a picture from her local community services outlet on social media. The "free shoes" section had zero pairs of shoes—the only thing on the shelves was a sign pleading for donations.

If the idea of stepping outside your comfort zone (and your

tightly packed schedule) leaves you cold, consider this: Volunteers feel great about themselves. They have a sense of purpose. They feel appreciated. And they are never bored. Ask any volunteer, and he or she will tell you there is nothing quite like doing something good for a stranger in need.

The good you do doesn't need to be a lifetime commitment either. You can volunteer to coach soccer for a couple of months every spring or summer. Serve meals to the needy each Thanksgiving and Christmas. The important thing is to try something. Leap over your objections just one time and see how it feels.

A friend I will call Ray tried this. He reluctantly agreed (with his kids) to help deliver presents to needy families one Christmas. His reluctance stemmed from the fear he would miss two hours in the gym he had been looking forward to.

When he and his band of volunteers arrived at an apartment complex, they found the sidewalks and stairs encased in ice. A quick canvass of various tenants produced only one plastic snow shovel—no match for the thick ice. However, one tenant noted, "I do have this steel hammer..."

Armed with the hammer, Ray smashed ice for two hours, alternating right and left hands. When it was all over, he had completed a workout so grueling he could barely lift either arm. More important, the apartment's tenants could once again walk safely. Many of the tenants didn't own a car and walked to school, work, and the local grocery store.

"I learned something about volunteerism that day," Ray recalls. "It's a gift that has a way of giving back. Between the gratitude of all those people and the awesome workout I got, I almost felt guilty."

I hope this story encourages you to volunteer. If you are worried it will steal time with your kids, bring 'em along!

"Unselfish and noble actions are the most
radiant pages in the biography of souls."

David Thomas

61

Speak Truth to Your Mind, Body, and Soul

Do not conform any longer to the pattern of this world,
but be transformed by the renewing of your mind.
Romans 12:2

I recently reconnected with my friend Denise. As we talked, she shared with me what she has been going through. She divorced recently, and she has three older children—the youngest is a high school senior. It was interesting to compare single-mom journeys with her. I learned that even when one's children are grown or almost-grown, divorce affects them deeply.

Writing this book has been difficult at times, but because of people like Denise, it has brought so much healing. God has blessed me in the process, and I know he has spoken to me through the single moms I talked with as I wrote.

Denise encouraged me so much when she reminded me, "We need to speak truth over ourselves. We need to forgive ourselves and start believing we deserve to heal. We really do!"

Denise's story is very painful, but through it all she has learned to lean on the Lord and believe what he says about her regardless of what anyone else may say. As we talked, she shared this Scripture with me:

Why, my soul, are you downcast?
    Why so disturbed within me?
Put your hope in God,
    for I will yet praise him,
    my Savior and my God.
My soul is downcast within me;
    therefore I will remember you (Psalm 42:5-6).

"In this psalm," Denise explained, "David gives us a prime example of what self-talk should look like. Our inner dialogue consists of up to 300 words per minute. That's up to 144,000 words we tell ourselves in just an eight-hour day! What we are speaking to our inner woman is vital to our emotional and spiritual health and maturity. This is why David prayed, 'Let the words of my mouth and the meditation of my heart be acceptable in your sight, O LORD, my rock and my redeemer' (Psalm 19:14 ESV).

"If we do not monitor what we are speaking to our hearts and minds, then our daily talk can cause us to stumble. It can stagnate our growth, freedom, and healing. Every action we take is based on our thought life. What we ultimately believe to be true propels our actions. It creates habits, forms our character, and sets the path for our future life circumstances."

As Denise shared, she impressed on me the fact that we must realize we can't believe everything we think or feel to be true. Our hearts are deceitful. Too often, we fall prey to untruths that need to be exposed for what they really are. We need to ponder what we believe to be true about ourselves and about God. Only the truth of God's Word can set us free from the prison of our minds.

As Denise puts it, "We must yield our thought life and self-talk to Christ. We must choose to trust God more than we trust our feelings. If something doesn't line up with the Word, then it is a lie. If we accept lies as truth, then we choose to reject God's truth. Meditating on biblical truth and being consistent in our prayer lives equip us with 'the sword of the Spirit, which is the word of God' (see Ephesians 6:17).

"There is a battle for control over our thought lives, and we are called to stand firm, to take up the armor of God, and to fight for truth. As we gain ground in this battle, we find life in its abounding fullness of joy and strength for mind, body, and soul."

So, single mom, let us follow David's modeling and examine the reasons for our despair. Be honest with God. Pour out your heart in prayer and repentance. Invite the Holy Spirit to be your Counselor, your Healer, and your breath of life. Then, speak the Word to your soul and choose faith over feelings, truth over lies. You will once again praise God for his faithful help!

> *Heavenly Father,*
> *I come to you with a grateful heart. Thank you for the Word you have given us. Thank you that your Word is still relevant today. I ask that the Holy Spirit will reveal your Word to me. Write your truth on the tablet of my heart and on my mind. I repent for believing lies, for trusting my feelings instead of standing on your truth. Lord, reveal the lies that I mistakenly believe to be truth. Weed them out of my*

heart and mind. Fill me and strengthen me with your Spirit so I can stand firm. I yield my thoughts to you. Give me faith. Help me to trust you and not to lean on my understanding. Give me a passion to seek you, to meditate on the Word, and to build my relationship with you in my prayer time. Show me your glory. Bring freedom, healing, and abundant life into this mind, body, and soul.

Amen.

In addition to the Scriptures noted in this devotion, Denise and I recommend these for your consideration, and meditation:

Psalm 116:7	Proverbs 16:3	2 Corinthians 10:5
Proverbs 3:5-6	Jeremiah 17:9	Ephesians 6:10-20
Proverbs 4:23	Romans 12:2	Philippians 1:6

62

You Are Gifted!

Get the word out. Teach all these things. And don't let anyone put you down because you're young. Teach believers with your life: by word, by demeanor, by love, by faith, by integrity. Stay at your post reading Scripture, giving counsel, teaching. And that special gift of ministry you were given when the leaders of the church laid hands on you and prayed—keep that dusted off and in use.

1 Timothy 4:11-14 MSG

*I*magine receiving a gift from a wealthy person who is renowned for her taste in selecting perfect (and expensive) presents for everyone on her gift list. Wouldn't this be a package you would be eager to open? A gift you would want to start enjoying right away?

Sadly, many people who have received gifts from the perfect Giver have never bothered to open them or use them for their intended purpose.

God has gifted each of us with abilities. And he never makes a mistake. His gifts are never the wrong size or style or inappropriate in any way. No one has ever needed to return a gift from God.

If only we will open God's heaven-sent gifts, we can use them to benefit others and bring glory to him. Do you know what your gifts are? (A sense of humor, a talent for art, culinary expertise, or the ability to encourage others? These are just a few of many.) Are you using your gifts? Or are they lying dormant, gathering dust? If this is the case, it's time to tear into that aging wrapping paper.

Putting your God-given talents to work is one of the most satisfying things you will ever do. As you do what God created you for, you gain a deep sense of purpose and become closer and more grateful to the One who gave you your talents. Few things are as beautiful as Creator and creation working together. So don't neglect your gifts. Don't wish you had someone else's. Do all the good you can with what you've been given.

God-given abilities are like muscles—either you use them or they wither and fade away. That's no way to treat a precious gift.

> *"In whatever way you can do so, according to the talents and gifts God has given you, you are to be salt, and light, and whatever part of the Body of Christ you were made to be. You need to tell us what's going on with you so the rest of the Body (of which you are a part) can work together with you."*
> —Chris Manion

63

God Blesses Those Who Persevere

As you know, we count as blessed
those who have persevered.
James 5:11

$f$ally didn't want to be a TV star. She just wanted to be on the radio. A correspondent or a disc jockey. She didn't have to be seen as long as she could be heard.

However, the recent college grad could not find a radio station that would hire her—in the entire United States. "No woman can attract a radio audience," she was told over and over.

So she broadened her search. She made her way to the Dominican Republic, where she found work as a radio reporter, covering political uprisings.

With some experience on her résumé, Sally returned to the United States to try her luck again. She did find radio jobs this time. The problem was *keeping* those radio jobs. She was fired from 18 stations. Things were so rough at one point that Sally found herself living in her car.

After firing number 18, Sally took stock of her life. She knew she wanted a life in broadcasting, but she wondered if she had the skills and personality for it. And she wondered if radio really was a man's world.

What's more, she was now in her late forties. Time was running short. It was hard enough for a woman to make it in radio; the odds were stacked against a middle-aged woman.

Then she heard about a job opening—host of a political talk show.

Sally knew virtually nothing about American politics. Still, she convinced the show's executives to give her a chance. Using her low-key conversational style, she hosted her first episode, sharing what Independence Day meant to her. She didn't speak from a vast knowledge of politics; she spoke from her heart. Then she invited listeners to call in and do the same.

The phone lines jammed. The show was an instant hit.

Within two years, Sally Jesse Raphael's radio talk show had moved to television, where it reached more than 8 million viewers in North America and the United Kingdom. For the next two decades, viewers tuned in to hear what the woman with the easy style and oversized red-framed glasses had to say.

During the Emmy-winning show's long run, Sally had plenty of chances to encourage her viewers to use every setback and failure to spur them on to something better, just as she had done.

She also insisted that a sense of humor is vital for enduring those hardships. She quipped, "You go to college, you get a master's degree, you study Shakespeare...and you wind up being famous for plastic glasses. Go figure."

Spoken like a woman who knows that one must face life's challenges with clear eyes (bespectacled though they may be), not through rose-colored glasses.

My mom and I are both fans of Sally Jesse Raphael. I find it particularly inspiring that she finally found career success in her forties—a time when many single moms are trying to make a new plan for their lives.

> *Heavenly Father,*
> *I confess I can get impatient with my life. I am working hard but not always seeing results. Please remind me your plan is good and your timing is perfect. Help me to be patient. Help me to persevere. Most of all, help me to remember that even when it appears nothing is happening for me and my family, you are always there, loving me and working in ways beyond my view and often beyond my understanding.*
>
> *I thank you for your preserving love.*
>
> > *In your name,*
> > *Amen.*

64

Tough Love

Make a careful exploration of who you are and the work
you have been given, and then sink yourself into that.
Don't be impressed with yourself. Don't compare yourself with others. Each of you must take responsibility for
doing the creative best you can with your own life.
Galatians 6:4-5 MSG

*P*arenting is *hard*."

I wish I had a dollar for every time I have heard these words
or uttered them myself when talking with my friends. Yes, parenting is gratifying, fun, and wonderful, but it's a challenge too,
especially when you feel so alone. In talking with other single
moms, I'm reminded that many of them miss having a partner
in their decision-making, especially the big decisions.

"Should we send our kids to public school or a Christian
school, or should we go the homeschool route?"

"Should we buy a house or rent?"

"Should we move to an area where the job market is better,
even if we have to leave friends and family behind?"

"What should we do about our kid who seems to be going
down the wrong road and doesn't respond to the disciplinary
measures recommended by the parenting experts?"

I know I'm not the only single mom who has second-guessed herself time and again about decisions large and small.

I recently discussed this challenge with Jennifer, a friend and a single mom of three. She told me, "Just this morning, I went in to wake up my youngest child for school and saw a closet overflowing with dirty laundry. I had asked my kids to do their laundry the night before. I did my best to fight the urge to start griping about that."

Jennifer couldn't vent to a partner or consult him about a plan. She was exasperated. She looked at her young son and said, "Well, I don't know what you are going to wear today, because your clothes are all dirty!"

Then she turned and walked out of the room.

A few minutes later, Jennifer's youngest appeared before her, dressed and ready for school. She was amazed.

"Boundaries are scary," she told me. "As a single parent, I fear what might happen if I stop taking responsibility for everything—if I fail to solve every single problem. I know I need to teach my kids responsibility, but I don't want to give them more than they can handle. For me, one of the scariest questions is, 'What will happen if I let them fail?'

"But you know what? My baby boy went to school wearing slightly dirty pants today, and the world did not come to an end. And I bet that next time he will do his laundry when I remind him to."

Jennifer's story was a timely reminder for me. When we are faithfully trying to raise our kids well, God has a way of rewarding our efforts.

"Lord Jesus, teach us to be generous;
teach us to serve you as you deserve—
to give and not to count the cost;
to fight and not to heed the wounds;
to toil and not to seek for rest;
to labor and not to seek reward,
except that of knowing that we do your will."

—Saint Ignatius of Loyola

65

Refuge

God, you're such a safe and powerful place
to find refuge!
You're a proven help in time of trouble—
more than enough and always available
whenever I need you.
So we will never fear
even if every structure of support were to crumble away.
We will not fear even when the earth quakes and shakes,
moving mountains and casting them into the sea.
For the raging roar of stormy winds and crashing waves
cannot erode our faith in you.

Psalm 46:1-3 TPT

*R*efuge. Just writing that word touches my heart. I visualize a mama bird with her feathers fluffed out as she covers her vulnerable babies with warmth and protection. These "bird moms" are determined. They make sure their babies are completely covered by their protective wings. They simply won't let any harm come to them. They strive to provide perfect refuge.

While writing this chapter, I looked up the word "refuge" in several dictionaries. I found definitions like "a condition of being safe" and "sheltered from danger or trouble."

The Bible features many verses about God's protection over

us. Here are a few of my favorites. I encourage you to meditate on these and to turn to them when you need to be reminded of God's care for you.

- "I will say of the LORD, 'He is my refuge and my fortress, my God, in whom I trust'" (Psalm 91:2).

- "Whoever fears the LORD has a secure fortress, and for their children it will be a refuge" (Proverbs 14:26).

- "You're as real to me as bedrock beneath my feet, like a castle on a cliff, my forever firm fortress, my mountain of hiding, my pathway of escape, my tower of rescue where none can reach me. My secret strength and shield around me, you are salvation's ray of brightness shining on the hillside, always the champion of my cause" (Psalm 18:2 TPT).

Years ago, I got to meet gospel singer Darrell Evans at a concert in Colorado. As we talked backstage, I invited him to come to my college (Savannah College of Art and Design in Savannah, Georgia) and conduct a praise and worship night with me. I wanted to create a large painting while he performed.

To my surprise, he said yes. I will never forget that night. He brought so much light to my school. He performed many of my favorite songs, including "Refuge" from his 1997 project *Let the River Flow*.

Many years have passed since that event, but I still love to listen to "Refuge." I enjoy playing it in the morning as I pray for the day ahead. The song inspires me to pray for my boys, that they will experience God's covering and feel protected throughout the day.

When I talk with other women who are single moms because of divorce, they often mention the absence of a man of God in the home—the protection of a husband and father. But songs like "Refuge" can remind us all that God can fill that role in our families. He is a husband to the husbandless and a father to the fatherless.

If you have never heard of Darrell Evans, I encourage you to check out the song "Refuge." Listen to it while reading Psalm 46 in your favorite Bible version. I know you will be encouraged.

Heavenly Father,
Thank you for your covering, for your protection.
You are indeed a refuge for my children and me.
Thank you, Lord, that I can lean on you to be my
Husband and my children's Father. I ask you to
give me the peace of refuge as I walk through today.
Remind me that my boys and I have a hope and a
future in you.

Thank you, Lord! In your precious name,
Amen.

66

Sunsets

> One thing I have asked of the LORD, and that I will seek:
> that I may dwell in the house of the LORD [in His pres-
> ence] all the days of my life, to gaze upon the beauty [the
> delightful loveliness and majestic grandeur] of the LORD
> and to meditate in His temple.
> Psalm 27:4 AMP

I have a talented friend who is an amazing photographer. She takes pictures of sunsets and posts them to social media. I absolutely love her pictures! I look forward to seeing them—I can't get enough of them. Maybe it is the painter in me, but sunsets always get to me. I am sure sunrises would wreck me too (in a good way) if I woke up early enough to see them. (Note to self: Wake up earlier to see more sunrises and start the day with this symbol of a fresh and beautiful beginning.)

I simply love the way God paints the sky. I am always intrigued by cloud formations and the lovely way the sun filters through them. I even love the way airplanes leave their cloud-like vapor trails in the sky. Many times, I will see that a cross has formed, and I take that as a sign from the Lord. I am reminded to "take it to the cross"—whatever *it* may be, whatever burden is weighing me down at the time. I find that basking in God's beautiful sky brings me a sense of calm.

At this point in my boys' lives, they are now well accustomed to my pulling our car off the road so I can capture a photo of the sky. When they can't abide one more diversion, I ask them to snap a shot out the window or through the sunroof, praying every second that they don't drop my phone.

I am proud to report, however, that both my boys share their mom's love for nature. I will be cooking dinner, and one of them will come running in the house, exclaiming, "Mom, you have to come and see the sky—right now!"

Of course, I stop what I'm doing and run outside. I don't want to miss God's latest masterpiece in the sky. Natural beauty brings us a sense of awe, of calm. I want my boys to seek this and appreciate it. I want them to enjoy every one of God's canvases.

This is one of my most fervent prayers: "Please, Lord, don't let my sons get distracted by the craziness of life. May they seek and find the incredible peace and joy and majesty of your creation."

Heavenly Father,
Thank you for your beauty. Thank you for the way the heavens declare your glory and the sky above proclaims your handiwork. Help my boys and me to take the time to find the calm, the quiet, that only you can give. Let us lie down in green pastures and beside still waters. Lead us on paths of righteousness for your name's sake.

Teach me to look at the little things that can speak to us. I pray for my children, that the love of your natural beauty will abide with them all the days of their lives. May they appreciate your creation and never get enough of your beauty. May they never get too busy to worship you.

> Thank you, Lord. In your name,
> Amen.

67

Self-Care

Cast your cares on the LORD
and he will sustain you;
he will never let
the righteous be shaken.
Psalm 55:22

*T*here are many kinds of single moms in today's world. I know moms who have been widowed at a very young age and decided not to remarry. I know lifelong single women who have decided to adopt. Living in Colorado, home to the Air Force Academy and several large US Army bases, I know moms who are alone for months at a time while their husbands are deployed around the world.

And then there are those of us who are single moms because of divorce.

Even though our circumstances differ, we share a common struggle: How do we care for ourselves so we can effectively care for our families? Recently, I discussed this challenge with my friend Angie Honeycutt, who is such a talented communicator. As we talked, I found her thoughts so relevant and so well rendered that I asked her to share them in the remainder of this devotion.

I don't know a single mom who doesn't struggle with the concept of self-care. We are such caregivers, so focused on others—especially our kids. But how do we take care of ourselves? The world says we have earned this right: "Go get your nails done, girlfriend. You've earned it!"

But I know myself better than that. I know the many ways I have failed. I know the people I have hurt. I know the messes I've made—and the ones I will continue to make. I'm not sure I've earned anything. Besides, nothing I could ever earn would equal what Christ did for me on the cross. The debt he paid for me in a radical, unbelievable act of love.

So, no. I don't deserve the fancy nails. I haven't earned myself some soothing retail therapy, a Netflix binge, or an exotic vacation. I won't believe the lies. I haven't earned the right to pamper myself. I work hard to provide for my kids, not to get a material reward. Thanks, but no thanks.

Self-care is not about pursuing some kind of prize. Instead, we single moms should practice self-care because we *need* to. I get worn out. I am human. I am a mom who needs megadoses of radical love. When I practice a bit of self-care, I am not pampering myself; I am acknowledging to the world my utter weakness. I am admitting the need to recharge myself physically, mentally, and especially spiritually.

Sometimes I need to escape the house for a couple of hours—to get out in nature to spend time alone with my God or to go for a long run with a friend. This is way better than closing myself in my room and doing the "ugly cry" for an hour or more.

When I practice the right kind of self-care, I am confessing,

"Sweet Jesus, I don't have it all together. In fact, I am a mess today. I desperately need you. I need the love I know I don't deserve."

Please hear this, my fellow single mama: God loves it when we stop pretending and come to him with all our needs. We glorify him when we let it all go, when we finally admit, "My life is too much for me right now. I am too weak."

Here is a verse that changed single motherhood for me: "He said to me, 'My grace is sufficient for you, for my power is made perfect in weakness.' Therefore I will boast all the more gladly about my weaknesses, so that Christ's power may rest on me" (2 Corinthians 12:9).

Don't we all need this power Paul wrote about? I know I want it. And I need it. That's why I don't mind boasting to people in my life about my desperate need for the Lord.

So I don't look at self-care as a prize for all my effort. I see it as grace, and the Lord lavishes us with grace through his love and power.

In a world that shouts, "Earn it! Hustle so you can earn more and more!" Jesus whispers. He assures us, "You are loved. Be still. Be near me." Self-care is the Lord's invitation for us to slow down and tenderly care for our bodies, minds, and souls. The bodies, minds, and souls he loves so much that he left heaven to rescue and reclaim them.

"An empty lantern provides no light. Self-care is the fuel that allows your light to shine brightly."
Anonymous

68

Mad Skills

Consider the blameless, observe the upright;
a future awaits those who seek peace.
Psalm 37:37

*T*here are good reasons Abraham Lincoln tops many lists of most-admired presidents. He was willing to admit his mistakes. He had a sense of humor about his faults. And he lived out the courage of his convictions even when it put his life in danger.

But one of the traits I admire most is President Lincoln's ability to handle conflict, especially when that conflict was infused with anger. Here is just one example.

Edwin Stanton served as secretary of war for the Union during the Civil War. Part of Lincoln's "team of rivals," Stanton was unlike his boss in almost every way. Lincoln was calm, even in a crisis. Stanton was hot-tempered. Some compared him to an angry Old Testament prophet. Lincoln was good-natured and forgiving; Stanton was stern and unflinching in his standards for others.

At one point during the war, Stanton became enraged at a Union general whom he felt was defying his authority. Stanton shared his anger with the president. Lincoln listened patiently and then suggested that his secretary write a sharp letter, expressing exactly how he felt.

Stanton departed to write. His pen was like a hypodermic needle, injecting every drop of his anger into scathing words. He returned to Lincoln, brandishing the letter like a sword. The president read carefully. Then Stanton asked Lincoln for permission to send the letter.

"You don't want to send this letter to the general," the president advised. "You should put it in the stove. And now that you feel better and are less angry, write another letter. That's what I do."[5]

As you can see, one of Lincoln's hallmarks was his wisdom. And he was wise enough to know that angry people often say things they don't mean. Or they say things they do mean but in a cruel, nonproductive way. The message gets lost in the madness.

This is why Lincoln sometimes wrote two letters to address difficult people and difficult situations. He called them "hot letters" because the first draft ended up burning in a woodstove or being torn to bits and sprinkled like confetti into a waste bin.

Imagine what could happen if we thought about Abe Lincoln the next time we sat down to type an angry email to one of our kids' teachers or to an ex? What if we emulated this practice before stirring up a Tweet storm or responding to a cruel Facebook comment with one of our own?

We can do the same thing when we're ready to "go off" on someone on the phone or in person. We can think about what we're about to say and how we might say it. We can think about those wise words, "Do unto others..."

Yes, the Lincoln-esque approach to handling anger is not just presidential; it's biblical. The Bible doesn't command, "Never, ever get mad." It says, "In your anger do not sin."

Yes, everyone gets angry. Even a president. The key to effective harmonious relationships in our homes and beyond is to handle that anger appropriately. If you must blow off some steam, go ahead and do it. But do it alone. Make it the private rehearsal, not the public performance. That way, no one gets burned in the process.

We single moms are under a lot of pressure, and sometimes we feel we have a right to "lose our stuff." But what we say or do in anger cannot be unsaid or undone. To put it another way, it doesn't take much effort to place an unsent email in a trash bin. But it can take months to drag a damaged relationship out of one.

> *"I have always found that mercy bears*
> *richer fruits than strict justice."*
>
> —Abraham Lincoln

69

Drastic Measures?

The LORD does not look at the things people look at.
People look at the outward appearance, but the LORD
looks at the heart.

1 Samuel 16:7

*H*as this ever happened to you? You are at the pool, the beach, or the gym, and someone about your age walks by looking like a million bucks. Meanwhile, you are having one of those $9.99 bargain-rack kind of days. You think, *Woe is me*, and slink away because you don't feel like you measure up.

Isn't too much of modern life about measuring and rating? Dollars, cents, millimeters, miles, cubic feet, cups, pounds, percentages, degrees, and decibels. Ask just about any author, and he or she can tell you which book has earned the most five-star reviews on Amazon and similar sites. (And confess that those one- and two-star reviews are like punches in the gut.)

Of course, if we are going to measure anything, we need *some* kind of standard. But what happens when we try to measure our self-worth? After all, how do you assess a human being's value?

According to a *Wired* magazine article, if a human body were sold for each of its individual organs—a brain, a liver, a kidney, a pancreas—the price could total $45 million. However, if you reduced that same body to its basic elements and minerals (fats, water, sodium, and so on), you'd ring up only about 160 bucks.[6]

Now, my degree is in painting and illustration, not math, but it doesn't seem like money is a reliable indicator of human value. There are too many variables. Besides, whether you favor the higher or lower price tag, both figures represent how much a body is worth once someone is no longer using it—or at least not using certain parts of it.

Let's look at this topic from another angle. Think about *using* the bodies we are in right now to climb mountains, kayak, hug our kids, run through the sand, or savor an ice cream cone while basking in the sun. How can anyone put a price tag on that?

Our value is not determined by any person or institution, so likewise, it cannot be taken away or diminished by either. Our inherent, God-given worth trumps any labels, grades, or rating systems.

Being a great single mom, a trusted friend, a valued coworker—these are just as important as being a good world leader, movie star, or business mogul. And they are way more important than how you think you look next to that superwoman at the gym!

God loves you. He values you immensely. This is the truth, and we function most effectively when we walk in truth. Because the truth sets us free.

Creator God,
I confess that I can become too focused on questions
like "How do I compare?" and "How do I rate?" It's
an easy trap to fall into: letting how I stack up in

terms of salary, fitness level, or social-media popularity determine my self-worth. Please remind me that my true value cannot be measured by any human-made system. I have inherent value because I am your child and you love me.

Thank you for loving me. Thank you for giving me not only value but also a divine purpose in my life.

In your name I pray,
Amen.

70

Pinterest Moms

Since we live by the Spirit, let us keep in step with the
Spirit. Let us not become conceited, provoking and
envying each other.
Galatians 5:25-26

*C*an we get real about Pinterest for just a few minutes? Pinterest
is a great way to find recipes, craft ideas, and various fun house-
hold projects. Pinterest is an amazing tool, especially for us moms
who are always on the lookout for ways to make our families' lives
easier and more enjoyable—and making our homes warm and
wonderful places to be.

Unfortunately, Pinterest (and other social-media sites) can
also lead us into the comparison trap.

I like Pinterest because I am an artist—and a procrastinator.
(We'll talk more about the latter, but not right now. Maybe *later*?)

Anyway, the artist in me loves to do something special for my
boys' birthday parties or classroom celebrations at their schools.
I love to make cupcakes, cookies, or other special goodies. If
my sons request it, I try to make it happen. However, I can
make things harder than they need to be. I dive into the internet and quickly get overwhelmed by the possibilities: fancy fon-
dants, unusual frosting flavors, spectacular color schemes...you
name it.

My boys and I also binge Netflix, studying the various cooking shows and cupcake competitions, all in search of the next great creative idea.

All of this is simply not good for a person who is creative but also a perfectionist. I will mix, cook, and decorate late into the evening—anything to ensure that the little critter on my cake has perfectly sculpted whiskers. I have been known to throw out my first two batches of homemade frosting because they just weren't quite amazing and delicious enough.

I tell myself that the effort is worthwhile because I love to see my boys smile. I love it when they are proud of me, the mom who never resorts to store-bought goodies the way some other time-pressed parents do. I love taking cookies or cupcakes into the boys' classrooms and watch as they are quickly devoured. When I see kids smile as they bite into my latest concoction and hear the oohs and ahs, I'm convinced that all the time researching, baking, and re-baking was worth it.

But even though some kids might say that my fondant is a work of art, I suffer from Pinterest envy. My friend Kami regularly posts her handiwork online, and her Pinterest parties put mine to shame. She is the Pinterest mom that other Pinterest moms yearn to be. Every detail is on-point—the napkins, the straws, the customized goodie bags, the decorations, and so on. She even makes sure her outfit color-coordinates with those of her kids!

My older sister, Vania, is similarly gifted. She hosts teas for her friends and her Bible-study group, and every detail is so well-conceived. Every design element and every refreshment is impeccable. When I see my sister's handiwork, I start to think, *I'm not good enough. I don't do enough. I just don't have Vania's eye for detail!*

This brings us back to the trap I mentioned earlier. Pinterest and other social-media sites lead to comparison, and comparison leads to disappointment. As single moms, we struggle to find contentment in our busy lives. When you factor in the way comparison forces us to focus on our flaws, it's no wonder that so many of us are not living in joy the way we should. There is always going to be a mom who seems more organized than I am. Other moms will have more discretionary time or discretionary income than I do.

God doesn't want me to live like this. He doesn't want that for you either. He wants us to stop focusing on how we stack up to other moms and start focusing our thoughts on him. A while ago, I heard a woman share that when she sees anything on social media that tempts her to start comparing herself with a peer, she stops comparing herself with that person and starts praying for her instead. I realized this is a better way forward.

Why not ask God to bless another mom's efforts? Why not be thankful there are so many moms out there who are striving to create memories for their kids and show them how much they are loved?

Praying for others always helps me take my eyes off myself—and praise God with a thankful heart. God has given each of us talents he wants us to use. Let's encourage each other instead of one-upping each other. I have found that gratefulness is the perfect antidote to envy.

My generous God,
Thank you for the talents and resources you have
provided for me and my family. Help me to live a
generous life and share what I have to the best of my
ability. Keep me from the trap of comparing myself
with others. Set my eyes on you and you alone; set
my heart on gratitude.

Amen.

71

Decisions, Decisions, Decisions

Teach us to number our days,
that we may gain a heart of wisdom.
Psalm 90:12

I was hiking with a dear friend the other day and found myself talking with her about one of the hardest aspects of single motherhood—making decisions on my own. From the simple (what to make for dinner) to the difficult (whether to uproot my family and move to a better job market), these choices can be challenging.

I miss having someone to discuss things with, to bounce ideas off. When I was married and faced a big decision, I could get input; I could offer input. There was a shared responsibility, so all the pressure wasn't placed on one person's shoulders. I confess that it has been incredibly difficult to face the daily reality that I am truly on my own for so many of the decisions that affect my boys and me.

In the months immediately after my divorce, I found myself feeling stuck and indecisive. I wasted so much time debating in my own head and lamenting the fact that I faced so many difficult choices alone.

As I poured out my heart, my friend said, "I've known you for a while now, and I want to tell you that even though you feel like you just can't decide on things, you've actually made lots of decisions. I've seen it happen. You're doing better than you realize, and I see you getting stronger in your decision-making skills."

After that hike, I returned home feeling so grateful for my friend and for the way she saw me. She understood my frustrations and my daily struggles to trust in the Lord. She reminded me that I never was truly alone—and never will be. The Lord is with me. He is my partner, and I can bring all my tough decisions and worries to him. He walks beside me on every step of my journey.

I am growing as a person. I am getting stronger. But on those days when my strength fails, I know Jesus is right beside me. His strength never wavers, and his wisdom never fails.

Precious heavenly Father,
Thank you for being all I need during this challenging season of my life. Forgive me for trying to do this on my own understanding and failing to come to you with my decisions, for not trusting you with all my heart. Lord, please walk with me today. I want to communicate with you about every decision—even the little ones. I trust you with my life. I trust you with my boys' lives. You see my whole journey...beginning, middle, and end. I don't need to see that whole journey. I just need to walk with you, step by step.

In your holy name,
Amen.

Epilogue: The Art of Running

> Since we are surrounded by such a great cloud of witnesses, let us throw off everything that hinders and the sin that so easily entangles. And let us run with perseverance the race marked out for us, fixing our eyes on Jesus, the pioneer and perfecter of faith.
>
> Hebrews 12:1-2

*B*ack in January of 2012, I was reading *Runner's World* magazine, and I encountered an article that changed my life.[7] The article told the story of Julius Achon, a former Olympic runner from Awake, Uganda. At age 12, Julius was kidnapped by the Lord's Resistance Army (LRA), a militant group that was rebelling against the Ugandan government. He was forced to become a child soldier, but he escaped a few months later and returned to his village.

He returned to school and took up running. By age 17, he had attracted the attention of Ugandan sports officials. He was entered in the 1994 World Junior Championships in Portugal. Competing in shoes for the first time, he won the 1,500 meters, bringing his country its first-ever gold medal at the World Junior level.

Julius went on to represent Uganda at the 1996 and 2000 Olympic Games, serving as team captain both times. A few years later, while training near his home, he encountered a group of 11 orphans huddled under a bus and took them into his home. This effort formed the foundation for the Achon Uganda Children's Fund, an effort to provide health care and education for Uganda's children, many of whom have been left without family during the country's long civil war. As part of this effort, Julius wanted to create a health clinic that would provide care for his local village and the surrounding area.

Months passed, and I could not get that *Runner's World* article out of my head. I felt that I somehow needed to be a part of the mission. But I wondered how I could help. I am an artist, not a carpenter or a doctor or a fund-raiser. As strange as it might sound, the Lord revealed to me what I could do: Travel to Uganda and paint a mural in the health clinic's waiting room. I wanted to help the clinic be a warm, inviting place, especially for children.

Another part of my motivation was my mom. She was born in the Congo, and I had always wanted to see Africa, the land she calls home. She was such a huge help in preparing me for what I would face there. My mom continues to inspire me and impart wisdom to me every day. I am so grateful to have such a generous, godly, and loving woman as a role model! (Lord, thank you for my mom!)

I will never stop giving thanks for how my mom and dad have always supported me and encouraged me to pursue my dreams and passions. This African endeavor was no exception.

The clinic's grand opening was scheduled for August 25, 2012, which created a huge problem. My boys started school on August 22. Eli would start kindergarten, riding a school bus for the first time. Given the logistics of travel to Africa, I would have to miss this important family event. At another time in my life, I might have given up hope for my plans, but something told me I needed to take advantage of the opportunity *now*. (I wouldn't fully understand this feeling until years later.)

My mother-in-law at the time volunteered to venture to Colorado to help her son (my then-husband) with the kids, which was a big blessing to me. I felt more and more confident this was part of God's plan for me. I was still anxious about leaving home, but I was also eager to see how things would unfold. I told my sons that even though I would be far away for a bit, our hearts were all connected through God. That's a bond that can never be severed.

A few months before my flight, I began researching and planning my mural. I wanted to include the Ugandan flag and the gray crowned crane, the country's official bird. I researched the local language, Luo, so I could hand-letter the words "hope," "peace," "love," "renew," "strength," and "healing." And I knew I wanted to feature Micah 6:8: "What does the LORD require of you? To act justly and to love mercy and to walk humbly with your God."

When I arrived in Uganda, I knew I wanted to stay in the village while I worked. The people there informed me that I was the first Muzungu (white person) ever to stay there. I took six days to complete the mural, and it was by far the easiest one I have ever done even though I had to stand on a plastic chair that was perched on a coffee table to work on the top part of my design. And even though I had up to 50 people watching me every day. I hate painting with anyone watching. As a perfectionist, I like people to see the finished product, not the process with all its mistakes.

But none of that mattered this time. (By the way, if you would like to see the mural and the creative process behind it, visit becksafrica.blogspot.com.)

When I wasn't painting, I found other ways to serve. As I have noted, I played soccer in high school and college, so I brought three soccer balls with me and played with the local kids every evening. I love how sports can be a universal language. Our "pitch" was composed of rocks and sun-dried bricks, and the kids played barefoot. Many of them had never been taught the game—never even watched a match on TV—but they were just unbelievable players. I was amazed at their skill but even more so at the pure joy they experienced.

On my last night in the village, a translator helped me teach the kids hook 'em, a cat-and-mouse type of game that I learned years ago in church youth group. I think the locals enjoyed this almost as much as the soccer.

I attended church in the village and got to share a few thoughts in Luo. But for me, the highlight of the worship service was the dancing. These people danced like crazy before the Lord. I felt like the angels were right there with us as we praised the Lord. I wish churches in the United States had this kind of fire. It was amazing to see these Africans celebrate in the Lord. I think they are onto something!

The Kristina Health Care Clinic (named for Julius's mother) celebrated its grand opening on August 25, 2012. We had a worship service—and more dancing. Uganda's minister of health attended and gave a beautiful speech. All told, more than 3,000 people came to celebrate with us. I asked the many people who helped me during my visit to provide handprints to one of the clinic's walls. And because Julius, the Olympic runner, was the genesis of the whole thing, he provided his footprints in the colors of the Ugandan flag.

Today, the Kristina Health Care Clinic serves hundreds of sick and injured patients every month. I hope and pray my mural helps to brighten their experience.

Here is what I hope you, my single-mom friend, will take from this story. God places a variety of talents in each of us. You may be a teacher, musician, writer, athlete, health-care professional, or artist. I encourage you to listen for God's voice, his call for you to do something for him, even if it's something scary. Even if the timing seems all wrong. Sometimes we need to act *now*.

When I was planning to go to Africa, some might have looked at my circumstances and questioned the timing. Both my boys were very young, and I would be missing Eli's "first day of kindergarten" milestone. But now I am glad I seized that opportunity when the right pieces were in place to make it happen. When the Lord puts something in your heart, the Holy Spirit prods you and gives you passion for your task. And God will work out every single detail, whether you are a single mom or not. Honestly, I really didn't have much anxiety about leaving my boys, even though it was *hard*. I was at peace because I knew going now was the Lord's calling on my life.

Along these same lines, I know a few other single moms who

wanted to write a book like this one. They thought about it, and a couple of them even started working on proposals. Several months passed, and as of this book's print date, they are all either remarried or engaged.

As for me, this matter is in the Lord's hands, and I rest in that. I believe that if God calls you to remain a single mom, you need to bloom in that role. I have been living the single-mom life for more than two years now, and I want to continue sharing what I am experiencing (and learning!) with other single moms. As I mentioned in the introduction, this book has been a challenge. In many ways, it's not the best time to be writing a book, especially for a novice author. But it's the *right* time. I know that.

Sometimes, my friends, "waiting on the Lord" means *not* waiting.

> *"I have survived several deaths in my lifetime.*
> *My dad would always tell me, 'Do something*
> *for people, and God will spare your life.'"*
>
> —Julius Achon

Notes

1. R.A. Cummins, "The domains of life satisfaction: An attempt to order chaos," *Social Indicators Research* 38, no. 3 (January 1996), https://www.researchgate.net/publication/226181403_Cummins_RA_1996_The_domains_of_life_satisfaction_An_attempt_to_order_chaos_Social_Indicators_Research.

2. Robert A. Emmons and Heather A. Kaiser, "Goal Orientation and Emotional Well-Being," in Leonard L. Martin and Abraham Tesser, eds., *Striving and Feeling* (New York: Psychology Press, 1996).

3. Mark Moring, "Rock Star," *Christianity Today*, Christianitytoday.com/iyf/truelifestories/interestingpeople/8.52.html.

4. Jamie Martin's art-detective work has been covered by a variety of news sources, but I recommend Armando Veve, "How Science Uncovered $80 Million of Fine Art Forgeries," *Wired*, December 20, 2016, www.wired.com/2016/12/how-to-detect-art-forgery.

5. Paul F. Boller Jr., *Presidential Anecdotes* (New York: Oxford University Press, 1996), 135.

6. See "What Is Your Body Worth?" DataGenetics, http://www.datagenetics.com/blog/april12011; and Scott Carney, "Inside the Business of Selling Human Body Parts," *Wired*, January 31, 2011, https://www.wired.com/2011/01/ff_redmarkets/.

7. Charlie Shoemaker, "Born to Run Back," *Runner's World*, August 11, 2016, https://www.runnersworld.com/runners-stories/a21750581/born-to-run-back/.

About the Author

Rebecca List-Bergeron is a professional artist and designer and the author of *Faith Outside the Lines*. She graduated with honors from Savannah College of Art & Design, earning a bachelor of arts degree in painting and illustration. Becky lives in Colorado with her two sons, Caedmen and Eli, and her Siberian husky, Keva.

Create Space for Your Faith to Grow

If you're ready for the next fun step in journaling, *Faith Outside the Lines* is the creative pursuit you have been craving. It's filled with faith-affirming activities to nurture your heart, mind, and soul, such as...

* Cover this page in love—using words, pictures, symbols, scents... or anything!

* Fill this page with blessings. Then count 'em all up.

* When you see the word "God," what comes to mind? Fill in this page with your thoughts, feelings, and prayers.

These and many more engaging ideas await you in this unique interactive journal. Accept this invitation to go outside the lines and discover a deeper connection with our God of creativity and love.

To learn more about Harvest House books and
to read sample chapters, log on to our website:

www.harvesthousepublishers.com

HARVEST HOUSE PUBLISHERS
EUGENE, OREGON